Putting Work in Its Place

A VOLUME IN THE SERIES

Collection on Technology and Work

edited by Stephen R. Barley

Between Craft and Science: Technical Work in the United States
    edited by Stephen R. Barley and Julian E. Orr

Talking about Machines: An Ethnography of a Modern Job
    by Julian E. Orr

*Finding Time: How Corporations, Individuals, and Families Can Benefit
from New Work Practices*
    by Leslie Perlow

Putting Work in Its Place

A Quiet Revolution

PETER MEIKSINS

and **PETER WHALLEY**

ILR PRESS *an imprint of*

CORNELL UNIVERSITY PRESS   Ithaca and London

First published 2002 by Cornell University Press

Printed in the United States of America

Library of Congress Cataloging-in-Publication Data

Meiksins, Peter, 1953–
    Putting work in its place : a quiet revolution / Peter Meiksins and
Peter Whalley.
        p. cm.—(Collection on technology and work)
Includes bibliographical references and index.
    ISBN 0-8014-3858-6
    1. Hours of labor—United States. 2. Professional employees—United
States. 3. Women employees—United States. 4. Work and Family—United
States. 5. Part-time employment—United States. I. Whalley, Peter. II.
Title. III. Series.
    HD5124 .M45 2002
        306.3′61—dc21   2001005803

Cornell University Press strives to use environmentally responsible
suppliers and materials to the fullest extent possible in the publishing
of its books. Such materials include vegetable-based, low-VOC inks
and acid-free papers that are recycled, totally chlorine-free, or partly
composed of nonwood fibers. For further information,
visit our website at www.cornellpress.cornell.edu.

Cloth printing   10 9 8 7 6 5 4 3 2 1

To Joyce Mastboom, Robin Meiksins, and
Pam, Nick, and Ned Whalley

Contents

Foreword

Temporal pioneers and rebels move among us, living incognito in single-family homes on quiet streets in suburban neighborhoods, in the duplexes and apartments of bustling cities, and even on an occasional farm. Bearing little resemblance to the pioneers of America's past, they are just as surely blazing trails into territories where many of us hope someday to settle. Nor are they the sort of reformers on whom we have traditionally pinned our hopes and fears of social change. They do not demonstrate, form movements, or even speak out publicly. Yet, as surely as the woman suffragists and the unionists of the last century reshaped our social landscape with their bravura, the men and women whose lives are described in this book are fighting skirmishes, however private they may be, with corporations (if not our very culture) for the right to choose how we will allocate the time of our lives.

In recent years, scholars and journalists have written much about the time bind that shackles contemporary Americans, and the discussions have struck a nerve, especially among the middle classes. The general consensus is that Americans of all sorts are overworked and saddled with so many obligations that we no longer have time to enjoy our lives as we thought we would. The problem appears particularly acute for working women, on whom a disproportionate share of child care and household work still falls. Commentators have seized on this temporal malaise with a variety of purposes: to underscore continuing gender inequities in U.S. society, to highlight the tyranny of modern employment, to develop recommendations for public policy, and even to promote schemes and technologies for managing time more efficiently. Yet few researchers have explored what people actually do once they decide they've had enough and intentionally set out to restore balance between work and everyday life. Meiksins and Whalley address this void. Their objective is to help us to understand what people are doing to regain control of their time by reducing the number of hours they work without sacrificing either work or family and how they make sense of their experience. Aside from the fact that Meiksins and Whalley's research is timely and important, we include their book in the Collection on Technology and Work because the temporal dissenters they studied were technical professionals: engineers, software developers, and experts in information technology.

There is irony in the fact that technical professionals are, however unwittingly, in the front lines of the quiet revolt to redraw the temporal boundaries of our lives by putting work in its place. A hundred years ago and often just as unwittingly, technical professionals were busy helping organizations forge the temporal bonds that gradually made organizational men, and later women, of us all. That engineers and technical professionals should now be the ones to struggle with organizations over breaking those bonds may strike some as poetic justice. But as Meiksins and Whalley note, that engineers and software developers should lead such change should, on reflection, come as no surprise, especially to sociologists of work. At this point in history, technical professionals are perhaps better positioned than any other group to agitate for change in the culture of work, even if only as individuals. Bolstered by a strong allegiance to the quality of their craft (what the authors call the "work itself") and a healthy dose of cynicism about organizational politics and managerial careers, technical professionals possess crucial and relatively scarce skills without which the information economy would grind to a halt. Although they do not act collectively, technical professionals possess a kind of substantive bargaining power with employers that members of few other occupations enjoy, bargaining power reminiscent of the nineteenth-century tradesmen who built and maintained the tools of the last industrial revolution.

For those of us who study technical professionals up close, another irony is to be found in the pages of this book. For years managerial theorists have tried to convince us that most engineers view engineering as a springboard into management, despite the fact that since the 1960s survey after survey has shown that only a third of the engineering labor force harbors such aspirations. What engineers know all too well is that moving into management has long been the only option for achieving remuneration commensurate with their contributions to a firm. But as technical skills have become increasingly central to the entire economy and hence relatively scarce, engineers and other technical professionals have found alternatives. One is to move (or to threaten to move) from company to company to bid up one's salary and the challenge of one's work. Another path, albeit less well traveled, is to trade on the demand for one's skill to pioneer an employment contract more conducive to a well-rounded life. Meiksins and Whalley's informants are of the latter group.

The men and women who speak to us from these pages instruct us on the rewards and difficulties of being a temporal pioneer in a corporate landscape. To their credit, the authors share the same agenda that motivated their informants to participate: to disseminate the informants' hard-won lessons, their maps if you will, so that others may more easily follow in their footsteps. The last chapter of this book, in particular, inventories strategies and tactics for those who also seek temporal balance without sacrificing meaningful and interesting work. But along the way, Meiksins and Whalley present data that are instructive on other counts. I shall mention only one particularly provocative finding: that women were more successful at negotiating part-time and job-sharing arrangements than were men, who typically had to become independent contractors to achieve temporal flexibility. Although the difference points to gender inequities that continue to govern life in organizations, it also highlights how employees can sometimes use organizational policies to subvert other aspects of the system that the policies bolster. Most of the women who worked part-time initially used maternity leave as their rationale for negotiating the arrangement. Although employers may sanction maternity leaves as a nod to family life, if for no other reason than to comply with the Family and Medical Leave Act, with varying degrees of success the women in this book were able to use those policies to get their foot in the temporal door. Once they had worked part-time under sanctioned conditions, their employers were more likely to extend the arrangement. Without doubt it is unfair that men are not allowed an equal opportunity to reconfigure the temporal parameters of their lives. It is also surely true that the distinction helps to perpetuate stereotypical views of men and women of the corporation. Yet Meiksins and Whalley's informants ask us to pause long enough to think through other implications.

If both men and women must wage a guerrilla war against the dominant culture of employment to regain temporal balance without losing access to challenging work, doesn't it make sense to embrace whatever weapons you can use? Whatever else one may think, the women at least had a tool for negotiating greater freedom within the confines of an organization, and from a long-term perspective, perhaps their ability to manipulate the system is to be celebrated. For if the work of a pioneer is to find ways for the rest of us to make our way to territories that promise a better life, shouldn't we expect multiple routes, some of which seem more distasteful than others? In the process of getting from here to there, the arriving may sometimes outweigh the hardships of the going. Whether this is the case with respect to paths to reduced hours of work remains to be seen. What is incontestable is that most of the technical professionals who told Meiksins and Whalley their stories believed the arriving was worth the journey. Ultimately, the ethnographer's job is to give voice to the informants' views, not to criticize them. As you will see, Meiksins and Whalley have done the ethnographer's job well.

STEPHEN R. BARLEY

Acknowledgments

We began this project with a longstanding interest in technical work and a growing focus on the emergence of independent contracting and freelance work. We might have restricted our study to this area had it not been for the Alfred P. Sloan Foundation's burgeoning interest in work-family issues. It is not often that social researchers, particularly those who do qualitative research, receive an unsolicited invitation from a foundation to submit a research proposal. And when Hirsch Cohen called to wonder whether we might also be interested in part-time professionals, we were happy to listen. We are glad we did. We think the study is much richer because of the suggestion. We are grateful to the Alfred P. Sloan Foundation for its interest in our work and its generous support of this project. In particular, we thank Hirsch Cohen and Kathleen Christensen, each of whom provided both encouragement and invaluable suggestions at various points along the way.

One of the great pleasures of working on this book was the opportunity to meet and talk with a wide variety of intelligent and enthusiastic engineers, computer professionals, and technical writers. They were consistently willing to talk frankly with us about their lives, to help us locate potential respondents, and to share with us their astute observations. We owe a great deal to the many people whose experiences we report in this book.

We also owe a debt of gratitude to the audiences who responded to our presentations of preliminary versions of the arguments presented here and to the many colleagues who provided us with critical comments. In particular, we thank Cynthia Negrey, Sarah Matthews, and Judith Wittner.

We would not have been able to complete this project without the assistance of a variety of graduate students and co-workers. We are especially indebted to Jeffrey Fallon, Mary Wagner, Phyllis Clark, Patricia Robertson, Angela DeBello, Lynn Higgins, Victoria Russo, and particularly Andrea Girardi.

Fran Benson of Cornell University Press and Steve Barley, the editor of the collection in which the book appears, were enthusiastic about this project from the start and patiently awaited its completion. The book has been enriched by their excitement about its arguments and by their insightful criticisms and suggestions. Barbara Salazar worked hard to ensure the book has a modicum of readability. Dave Prout was wonderfully precise (and prompt) in preparing an index.

Finally, we too have lives that include but are not limited to professional work. Our families willingly joined us in discussing how work and other activities are and should be combined. They also tolerated the intrusion of this project into their lives and provided us with both encouragement and support. And they reminded us, from time to time, that a book, like other work, needs to be kept in its place.

Putting Work in Its Place

Introduction

When we called Andrea Cisneros to schedule an interview for this book, she was apologetic.[1] One of her two children was sick, her husband was out of town on business, and she had a project at work that was running late; could we come to her home at lunchtime and talk while she grabbed a bite to eat? We offered to call again later but she insisted that she wanted to talk to us. She told us it was important that more people got to know about customizing work time—a term we had used in the flyer we had sent her. "If I wasn't working part-time," she said, "I wouldn't be able to do this." Andrea was a manager on a job-share in the R&D department of a major electronics company located in a Chicago suburb. When we arrived at her upscale suburban house for the interview, the sick child was asleep and the older one had just gone back to school after walking home for lunch. Despite the work that clearly goes into looking after two children, especially when one of them is sick, Andrea wanted to tell us only about what a difference her job-share had made to her life. She told us that she had worked full-time when the elder one was younger, but "I missed him and every time he got sick, it was awful. If I went to work, I was miserable and felt guilty. If I stayed at home, then nothing got done at work. Now my job-share partner and I try to cover for each other. I can enjoy being

---

1. We will use the editorial "we" throughout, even when referring to situations that applied to only one of us. All the names of respondents are pseudonyms.

with the kids and not be frazzled and can enjoy the work at the same time. It's great."

Andrea's comments, at first, seem familiar. She sounds a lot like the kind of person proponents of family-friendly policies have in mind—a young mom who needs a temporary respite from work-family conflict. But as we listened to her talk, we began to notice something more: she talked about enjoying both work and kids, not just scrambling to get through the day. And as we talked with others, we kept hearing the same kind of thing.

We were particularly struck by the similarity between the sentiments of parents and people who were not parents. We talked to older professionals making the transition to retirement and younger professionals pursuing dreams in addition to their work. Some were independent contractors, others company employees working reduced time. All of them had interesting and enjoyable technical jobs, but they all wanted something more. As one of them put it: "I went part time to get a life." For all of the people we met, this goal of having a life in which one could enjoy a variety of activities turned out to be at the heart of their story.

In many ways professional technical work—engineering, computer professions, technical writing—would seem an unlikely setting to study ways of reducing the pressures of work time. The public image of such work is dominated by young, driven professionals eating and sleeping with their work: work is play and play is work and families are nowhere to be found. There is some truth to the image. Studies from Tracy Kidder's *Soul of a New Machine* (1982) to Leslie Perlow's more recent *Finding Time* (1997), with numerous journalistic accounts of Microsoft and Silicon Valley in between, have documented that for segments of the high-tech professions, in certain settings and at particular points in the development process, life can take on the round-the-clock frenzy of college finals. Nevertheless, as we shall see, this is not the way it is for all: not in all places, not in all settings, and not at all times. The technical professions are diverse and becoming more so. While still largely male—with the partial exception of technical writing—they are facing an influx of women with their own set of expectations about workplace culture. Nor do all technical professionals work in Silicon Valley, whose workplaces are hardly typical of the American economy as a whole. The culture of the Midwest has long placed a different emphasis on work-family relationships than either coast. Moreover, just as most lawyers do not work in New York law firms, most technical professionals do not work in dot-com start-ups. Work time has a different meaning in the many settings in which technical professionals work, and there are as many strategies for managing it.

The 1990s saw a growth in demand for reduced work time. Whatever the exact cause of the so-called time bind, there is no doubt that many Americans now feel that they would like more balance between their work and the other things they want or need to do. Many—especially professionals and managers—would like to reduce the time they commit to work, though few are able to do so at present. This book is about some of those who have succeeded.

We talked to engineers, technical writers, and computer professionals, all of whom had succeeded in one way or another in deliberately reducing their time commitment to work and customizing their work arrangements. We know from them that they feel atypical: that they feel privileged to have managed to do what they do. We know from conversations with other technical professionals that many of them work in settings where they believe such customized work time is not available. Our respondents have sometimes paid a price for their success, but we can learn from them about possibilities and limitations, about opportunities, about motivations and about practices. Much of this book documents the individual strategies they used to gain control over the balance of time in their lives.

We focus on two distinct strategies for managing and reducing work time. The first is the conventional route—though unusual in professional settings—of corporate part-time employment. Engineers, computer programmers, and a very few technical writers have been able to negotiate part-time arrangements with their existing employers, often continuing in their previous jobs with fewer hours, though generally with reduced or no benefits. The second route is less traditional: independent contracting. These professionals are in business for themselves and contract with clients for their services. This choice has given some of them greater control over their destinies by providing a way to reduce the time they commit to work.

The people we talked with are pleased and satisfied with their decisions. They feel committed to their identities as technical professionals and enjoy the work they do. They are equally pleased with the satisfactions of parenting or their other nonwork choices. They have refused to choose between the two. Individually they have had great success, but customized work arrangements are not yet the norm. By looking closely at the motivations, strategies, and practices of these successful technical professionals who have managed to customize their own work-time arrangements, however, we can offer successful examples to others. We may also learn something about why it has proved so difficult to enable people to customize work time. The agenda for the next decade is to transform these individualized successes into a normal practice of customized work time that allows more people to put work in its place.

1

Time, Technical Work, and the Pursuit of Happiness

The 1990s saw a reawakening of the discussion about work time that had lain dormant since the 1960s. Paradoxically, much of the impetus at the beginning of the decade came from the high level of unemployment and predictions that new technologies might lead to a permanent shortage of work.[1] In Europe in particular, the debate about work sharing and training for leisure was reopened as part of a campaign to spread the work and reduce the unemployment then seen as a permanent feature of the capitalist scene. In many ways, this development was an extension of labor's long-term struggle to reduce the workweek. In France, a Socialist-led government took power in 1997 with the promise to reduce the workweek to 35 hours, with no loss in pay. While it stopped short of requiring such a reduction, it quickly enacted legislation creating incentives for employers to reduce the workweek. In other European countries, most notably Germany, collective bargaining resulted in significant reductions in the workweek; the 35-hour week was the norm in unionized sectors such as metalworking by the mid-1990s. Meanwhile, Dutch workers worked fewer hours per year than workers in any other industrialized country, in part because of government action to reduce the workweek, in part because of both political and informal pressure to make part-time work more widely available. In

---

1. For a review of some of the more radical literature on time, see Rifkin 1987, Sirianni 1991, Aronowitz and Difazio 1995, and Gorz 1985.

the Dutch case, the latter was also linked to efforts to achieve greater gender equity (i.e. to encourage paternal involvement in child care and to enable men as well as women to work part time), a goal shared by the work-reduction efforts in several Scandinavian countries (Hayden 1999).

In the United States, however, the theme with the most public resonance was the overstretching of the American family. Juliet Schor's *Overworked American* (1991) reinvigorated the long-dormant discussion of work time by arguing that American workers were working longer hours now than in the past, and longer than workers in virtually all other industrialized countries. Revealing the distinctive American focus on the distribution of time between work and family, Schor's calculations included unpaid domestic labor as part of total work time. In the aftermath of Schor's book, as individual incomes remained stagnant, Americans began to hear more and more stories about jobs that demanded 60- and 70-hour weeks and workers who combined multiple part-time or even full-time jobs to make ends meet. The sense that family life was suffering became pervasive.

Arlie Russell Hochschild (1989) had already written eloquently of the "second shift" that women had to put in at the end of a long day at work. The press was full of stories about overscheduled kids whose parents became perpetual chauffeurs, as well as horror stories of latchkey children making do while mom and dad were both at work (Holcombe 1998). Parents talked of the need to schedule "quality time" with their children, while pundits warned of a decline in participation in public life (Putnam 2000). Even skeptics about the increase in working hours recognized that many Americans felt overburdened and unable to devote enough time to family and community (Robinson and Godbey 1997). Some of this concern was undoubtedly part of a conservative backlash against the large-scale entry of women into male-dominated occupations, but there was a real sense of time shortage as families sought to cope with both new opportunities for leisure and self-improvement and ever-lengthening family work hours.

As the 1990s progressed and economic boom replaced recession, the Family and Medical Leave Act was finally enacted, and companies began to respond to the zeitgeist by introducing work-family policies that were supposed to make it easier for parents—in reality, most often moms—to accommodate family life. Implementation, however, was slow and often controversial. Some hailed these new policies as a step in the right direction and actively campaigned to make them both more available and more extensive. The debate even began to include men, as writers such as Scott Coltrane (1996) talked about the "new man" who wanted to take a more active role in parenting and who presumably would also need extra time.

Others, however, were not persuaded. Part-time work, offered as an alternative to women to allow them to step off the fast track temporarily to look after young children, was sometimes denigrated as a "mommy track" that would preserve traditional gender inequality and set back women's progression into high-flying careers (Schwartz 1989). Even supporters of family-friendly policies expressed concern that their implementation left something to be desired. Mindy Fried (1998) argued that the predominant corporate culture made it difficult for parents to take full advantage of even existing policies. At the end of the decade, Hochschild (1997) was arguing that many women and men were refusing to take advantage of family-friendly policies because they found work a more orderly and satisfying environment than an increasingly stressful home life.[2]

Not all rethinking of the conventional time package was centered on gender or family. The end of the compulsory retirement age encouraged people to think about making a gradual transition to retirement rather than taking a single drastic step. The idea of a "bridge" job, an occupation that would link full-time work and retirement, became familiar. People began to talk about second, part-time careers, or continuing to work at their old jobs on a reduced schedule or as consultants or independent contractors (Doeringer 1990). And in the high-tech sector, the countercultural image of many of its young practitioners bred talk of working on a new video game, communing with nature, or even working for social change as a complement to a flexible and often lucrative professional job. Perhaps work does not need to involve long hours and continuous careers. At least the question was now being asked.

---

2. Hochschild's own evidence does not really support this argument. Most of the people she talked with were reluctant to take advantage of a family-friendly policy because their immediate supervisors resisted that policy. Nonetheless, this is the "finding" of *The Time Bind* that entered into public discourse.

Changes at Work

Underlying this questioning of the "standard" employment practices were two structural changes in the American economy. The
first was the entry of large numbers of women into the labor force in
a way that strained the traditional division of unpaid labor in the
home. Fifty-four percent of all families and 59 percent of families
with children under six now have two earners. Mothers with children under six now have a labor-force participation rate of 65 percent. Coupled with this increase in participation has been an increase in the number of hours worked for these dual-earner couples:
from fewer than 78 hours per week in 1973 to more than 84 hours
per week in 1994 (Clarkberg and Moen 1998, Lopata 1994). The
hours are particularly long for dual professional couples (Jacobs and
Gerson 2000). Such changes have created an inevitable time crunch,
and it is from mothers—unsurprisingly, given the slowness of men
to take up an equal burden of parenting and domestic chores—that
much of the impetus to rethink work time has come.

At the same time the sense is growing that the orderly structure
of middle-class careers that has dominated the American economy
since the 1950s is coming unstuck. Downsizing, reengineering, and
outsourcing have remade the traditional standard package of permanent, full-time career employment, and have added new terms such
as "contracting," "temporary work," "employee leasing," "self-employment," "contracting out," and "home-based work" to the management vocabulary. Intensified international competition, coupled
with volatile markets and legislation that makes it costly to lay off
workers and cheap to contract out, have led employers to cut their
permanent workforce and increase their use of part-time, temporary, and contract labor (Pfeffer and Baron 1988, Smith 1990,
Sweeney and Nussbaum 1989). New technologies have also diminished the need for internal career labor markets to fill the ranks of
middle management, leading to a growing occupationalization of
the labor force: employees are hired for their particular skills to
meet particular, often short-term, company needs (Barley 1991,
Piore and Sabel 1984).

Meanwhile, globalization and the increased demand for round-
the-clock services and production have created a new demand for
flexible time and employment schedules. These "on-demand" or

"market-mediated" work arrangements are often called "contingent" because they all lack long-term corporate ties and security.
Most observers have been rightly pessimistic about the growth of
such work. Low wages, lack of benefits, absence of career prospects,
and pervasive insecurity place many such workers firmly in the sec-
ondary labor market.[3] Nothing we say in this book really challenges
this pessimistic conclusion about many low-wage contingent jobs.

Other such work, however, especially in technical and professional occupations, may tell a different story. Some futurists have
begun to suggest that the traditional organizational career is becoming obsolete, replaced by new forms of "boundarylessness" (Arthur
and Rousseau 1996, Hecksher 1995). New career structures involving frequent job changes, retraining, and periods of self-employment
have been portrayed as offering opportunities for more fulfilling professional lives. Not everyone is persuaded by these arguments, however, and there is evidence that many employees still value many
aspects of traditional organizational careers. But even those who
urge caution stress that the new "portfolio" work offers some real
benefits, as managers and professionals acknowledge when they
talk about the changes affecting them (Cohen and Mallon 1999).
Among the positive effects to which they point are increased feelings of control and freedom and a greater degree of balance in their
lives. Thus for managerial, professional, and technical workers, at
least, these new work arrangements may be better seen as flexible
rather than contingent, offering positive opportunities to challenge
the rigid time demands of the American workplace.[4]

Studying Technical Work

This is the context in which we sought to talk with people who
had created their own solutions to the so-called time bind. We
wanted to find out how a sample of contemporary employees man-

3. The topic of contingency has received extensive coverage: see, among others,
Belous 1989; Christensen 1988; Levitan and Conway 1988; Mangum, Mayall, and
Nelson 1985; Polivka and Nardone 1989; Sweeney and Nussbaum 1989; and Tilly
1991, 1996.
4. The late 1980s saw an extensive discussion of these issues; see, among others,
Christensen 1989, Mangum et al. 1985, Osterman 1988, and Smith 1990.

aged to create work environments that gave them time to do other things. Technical professionals were an ideal group on which to focus this inquiry.

First, technical occupations are a large and rapidly growing segment of the American workforce. The technical professions (in contrast to the much-studied but numerically unimportant medical and legal professions) are among the largest occupations of any kind in the United States. Moreover, they are located in growing sectors of the economy. There is every reason to expect that such work will continue to proliferate as the technology and information demands of the economy expand. If one wants to understand the workforce of the twenty-first century, as distinct from that of the nineteenth or twentieth, technical professionals are a good place to start.

Technical professionals also work in a variety of settings, from large corporations to independent home offices. And their employment is not confined to idiosyncratic work environments (such as the corporate law firm) whose practices are alien to the experiences of the vast majority of the workforce. On the contrary, their distribution across the economy suggests that their experiences are likely to be shared by a variety of employees, especially those whose employment depends on the possession of valued skills of various kinds.

It should also be emphasized that our choice of middle-class occupations was deliberate. Middle-class workers are hardly a small minority; on the contrary, they represent an enormous segment of the American population. Moreover, if we are to understand the impact of changing work realities on the contemporary workforce, it is important to focus on groups directly affected by those changes. It is among such families that these changes in the balance of work and family have been most dramatic. Dual-earner arrangements are nothing new for working-class and poor families, who have long been encouraged by economic realities to have more than one source of income. What is new is the fact that the middle-class family is now, as a unit, working longer hours and sending more members out to work.

Middle-class technical professionals also have resources and bargaining power in the labor market. Employers are more likely to define such employees as "core" workers. They have scarce skills that are in considerable demand and thus can ask for things not readily accessible to other kinds of employees. They are often difficult to replace and employers are generally reluctant to give up the substantial investment in training and career development they represent. Technical professionals are thus in a position to be pioneers in the field of employment relations, to demonstrate what is possible when employers have a reason to make changes. In a period in which unionized labor has little ability to exert effective pressure on employers, it should not surprise us if changes in employment practices originate among middle-class workers.

Technical professionals make an interesting case for another reason. The provision of technical expertise has usually been thought to require long-term, trusting relationships rather than a purely market-based exchange of pay for service. This assumption has led, traditionally, either to stable professional-client relationships or to the elaborate career package characteristic of the corporate professional. This "standard package" often includes well-laid-out career trajectories and high material rewards in return for a commitment to autonomous work and, often, to long and unpredictable hours of work. These stable relationships are usually organized to ensure that satisfactory work is performed despite the client/employer's lack of knowledge of appropriate procedures and standards.[5] It is what one of us, in previous work, has called the "trusted worker" model of technical employment (Whalley 1986). It might be thought, then, that any attempt to disrupt these patterns by using contractors or employing part-timers would pose particular difficulties. The converse also holds: if such flexibility can work in technical professions, it stands a good chance in other occupations as well.

Talking with People

Our first criterion for deciding which people to talk with was that they had reduced their work time in the pursuit of other agendas. Rather than "part-time" we preferred the term "customized work schedule" to cover a broader range of reduced work-time

5. This issue has been extensively discussed in the literature on the professions. Brint 1994 has an extensive review, but see also Larson 1977, Meiksins 1988, Whalley 1986a, and Williamson 1974.

arrangements. In addition to salaried part-timers, we talked with independent contractors who worked fewer than regular hours. We also talked with people who worked less than full-time over a more extended period, such as a year, but who scheduled their work to cluster their free time rather than spread it equally by day or by week.

Within this overarching parameter, our emphasis was on variety. We rejected the idea of a company study because we were looking for a variety of organizational settings, large and small. We talked with independent contractors as well as employees because we were interested in how flexibility could play out in a variety of employment relationships. We talked with men as well as women, though not with as many men as we would have liked. We also sought variety in our definition of technical professionals, including engineers, computer personnel, and technical writers, to provide diversity.

Engineering is the paradigmatic organizational profession in which customized work arrangements have traditionally been unusual. In recent years, however, corporate restructuring and particularly the increasing numbers of forced early retirements among engineers have made such arrangements more common. Engineering thus seems a good context in which to study the rise of flexibility within an occupation where an internal labor market and corporate employment have been the norm. And because there are very few female engineers, employers are more likely to be under pressure to develop mechanisms to accommodate and retain women of childbearing age (McIlwee and Robinson 1992).

Computer specialists and technical writers are both in less structured fields of employment. Software programming has already earned a folk reputation for deviance; it is thought of as the home of the hacker, the whiz-kid dropout, and the genius making a living electronically in the backwoods of Oregon. It is an occupation in which the kind of arrangement we are calling "customized" has a relatively long history. Although there are a few major employers of technical writers, these people, too, are historically likely to be employed by small firms or to be engaged in various kinds of nontraditional work arrangements (temporary, agency, part-time, contracting). The prominence of women among computer specialists and technical writers[6] increases the numbers of workers who may want various forms of flexibility but also reduces the difficulty of finding comparable replacement workers.

We found that these occupational boundaries are themselves highly flexible. We talked with technical writers who began their careers as chemical engineers and computer programmers, programmers who are called engineers, and engineers who work entirely with electronics. In the end, any occupational comparisons we originally intended succumbed to our respondents' insistence on customizing their occupational identities as well as their work time.

We conducted the interviews in Chicago and Cleveland for the simple work-family reason that this is where we live. Interviewing in two cities, however, did help us guard against the effects of a single large employer or local labor market peculiarities and also added diversity to the social settings of the people with whom we talked. Cleveland is a traditional industrial center, with a base in heavy industry, metalworking, and automobiles. Chicago, by contrast, has both an extensive electronics industry and a postindustrial service economy, although it retains a significant traditional industrial sector. The two cities differ also in both size and culture. Chicago is substantially larger than Cleveland and is a national and international center of economic and cultural life; Cleveland is a regional center and considerably smaller.

We found people to talk with by "snowball sampling." We contacted professional associations, networking groups, employers, agencies, and others involved in the hiring and placing of part-time and other contingent workers. We then relied on the contacts made this way to lead us to other people. We also advertised in local professional journals and on internet sites. We avoided extensive reliance on employers because of their tendency to micromanage the research protocol and our own experience with the distorting impact on responses when access is sponsored by the employer. We tried to find respondents who worked for themselves as well as

---

6. According to the Bureau of Labor Statistics, women as a percentage of each occupation in 1999 were: engineers, 10.6%; computer scientists, 31.1%; and technical writers, 60.2%. There are far fewer technical writers, however, than engineers and computer scientists.

those tied more directly to organizations. Unlike lawyers and medical professionals, practitioners in these fields have no professional associations or licensing boards that list their names, so it was impossible to generate anything like a random sample; instead we tried to talk with people in specific categories, such as women, older workers, parents, and those with a variety of outside interests.

In all, we interviewed 127 part-time technical professionals, 67 in Chicago and 60 in Cleveland. Of these, 65 were part-time corporate employers and 62 were independent contractors. The nominal occupational breakdown was 31 computer professionals, 64 engineers, and 32 technical writers, but these occupational data should not be taken too seriously. Not only had many of these people moved through these categories during their careers, but, particularly in the electronics sector, the title "engineer" was often used so broadly as to embrace the other two categories. Of those we talked with, 99 were women, 58 had children under five, and another 18 had school-age children only.

Such variety can be costly if one is seeking to analyze cause and effect. We talked with too many people in too many situations to be able to tease out which organizational situations were most amenable to customized work. We only know what our respondents told us about their varied experiences. But this is exactly what we sought. We wanted to find out how individual women and men, at different stages of the life cycle, have managed to find a way around the institutional structures that frame the "normal" work career: how they have done it, why they have done it, and how it has affected them. By listening to what these people had to tell us about fitting work into their lives, we hoped to be able to understand the possibilities and difficulties, the joys and disappointments inherent in trying to beat the time bind.

The core of the research was a series of in-depth interviews. We tried to explore the issues with a minimum of presuppositions and wanted to be particularly sensitive to gender issues in the structuring of these experiences. We used in-depth interviewing techniques long associated with qualitative sociological research, and more recently with feminist methodology, to try to gain an appreciation of the technical professionals' own self-understanding.[7] The inter-

---

7. For good reviews of this kind of methodological strategy, see DeVault 1990, Mischler 1986, and Spradley 1979. Just as we sought to be relatively nondirectional in our interviewing, so our analytic techniques sought to derive concepts from the

views usually lasted ninety minutes or more, and were conducted in respondents' homes or workplaces, or occasionally in a neutral site such as a restaurant.

Our priority in the interviewing was to focus on the meaning behind our respondents' actions. Too often studies of part-time work have focused on behavior, asking simply what workers and employers do: which workers make the move to part-time work, what the economic consequences of doing so are, how their productivity is affected, and so on. We sought to go beyond such matters to discover what part-timers think about their decisions. What does work mean to them, and does reducing their time at work indicate a decline in their commitment to work? How do they understand the nonwork activities they are trying to fit into their lives? Were these activities freely entered into, or had they felt compelled in some way to take on these tasks, so that they are only reluctantly working less? By allowing our respondents to tell us, in their own terms, what part-time work is and what it means to them, we sought to avoid placing part-time work in any preconceived category, instead letting our respondents provide us with concepts to make sense of their experiences.

The people we talked with were eager to discuss their experiences with reduced work arrangements. Many were evangelical on the subject. They wanted to tell us why they had customized their work time and how. They wanted others to know what to say to persuade managers to let them shift to part-time work, or how to retain clients while taking time off to travel. They spoke enthusiastically about their lives, emphasizing that they enjoyed their jobs and that they continued to think of themselves as engineers or technical writers or programmers. At the same time, they also stressed the pleasures of their roles as parents, volunteers, hobbyists, whatever. As we shall see, putting work in its place is not always easy, but it can be done.

------

research material rather than to fit the material into an a priori framework. By allowing the inductive coding of the material, we sought to generate the kind of grounded theory (Glaser and Strauss 1967) that would allow us to make better sense of the workers' experiences. Most interviews were taped and later transcribed for analysis. On occasion, however, for technical reasons—background noise, for example, or because of a respondent's reluctance to be taped—we had to rely on extensive notes taken during the interview.

Overview

In Chapter 2 we explore the variety of reasons the people we talked with gave us for wanting to reduce their working time. Contrary to the stereotype of the part-time professional as a young mother struggling to juggle job and children, we found a variety of rationales for seeking customized work. We also found that what people mean by "reduced work" and the processes by which they decide to become part-time workers vary considerably. This diversity points to the limitations of one-size-fits-all responses to the demands for part-time work.

In Chapter 3 we assess the impact of these choices on our respondents' perceptions of themselves and their work. Often criticized as being uncommitted to work or, if they have children, as being only part-time parents, the people we talked with insist on their identities as professionals even while pursuing other interests. In working part-time they are challenging not just institutional arrangements but the corresponding pressure to identify completely with those institutions. Instead of finding their identities in a single sphere, our respondents are creating much more open-ended commitments.

In Chapters 4 and 5 we turn to the actual practices by which our respondents manage to customize work time to fit their needs. In Chapter 4 we look closely at corporate part-timers and examine the way new procedures are negotiated, often around seemingly insurmountable obstacles. In Chapter 5 we do the same for independent contractors. While the two differ in some respects, we also note the fundamental similarities between organizational professionals and contractors who seek to reduce their work hours.

In Chapter 6 we look at practices in domestic life. For working mothers—and, by extension, working fathers, when they take parenting seriously—it is not enough simply to resist the "greedy institution" of work if they are to get a life: they also need to resist the equally greedy institution of the family. As we shall see, maintaining an identity as a mom requires as much rearranging of the traditional package of domesticity as being a part-time professional does that of work.

In Chapter 7 we examine one further challenge that our respondents are making to the conventional structuring of work time. When part-time professional work is considered acceptable at all, it has always been as a temporary solution to a limited problem. If we take our respondents' desires seriously, this assumption falls short of the mark. Instead of looking for a short-term solution to a limited problem, many of the people we talked with were seeking an extended rearrangement of working time; not a short-term arrangement but an ongoing customization of work time that would allow them to continue to create a satisfactory life as their desires and interests changed.

Finally, in Chapter 8 we provide suggestions, some for individuals, some structural, that may move us further along toward customized work time. As individuals seek to expand their range of choices, as they reconfigure what it means to have a career, pursue an avocation, or be a parent, institutions and workplaces will experience continuous pressure to adapt and become more flexible.

2

Choosing to Work Less

In 1938, organized labor won the battle for the 8-hour day. It was a hard-won accomplishment of the New Deal after a half-century of labor struggle. The struggle to manage work time, however, lost steam in the United States as labor came to be more interested in paid overtime than in increased time for leisure or to spend with family. The experience of mass unemployment in the Great Depression also caused American workers to equate leisure with unemployment; the more hours they could work, the better (Hunnicut 1988). By the late 1990s American work time was approaching that of Japan and far exceeding that of European societies.

Professional, managerial, and other "exempt" labor never even had the ability to restrict work time. Professional work continued to be organized around the image of the practitioner ever willing to meet the needs of the client, day or night (Seron and Ferris 1995), while managers were expected to display their commitment to the organization by a conspicuous gift of work time. Technical professionals, caught somewhere between the two images of profession and management, had both images to live up to. They were expected not only to display loyalty to the organization by working long hours but to enjoy doing so as they pursued their professional vocations.

For some technical professionals, of course, work *is* life. In the start-ups of Silicon Valley or the dot-coms of Chicago, dominated by young people in their twenties, one can find all the toys, the basketball hoops, the "nap tents" and other paraphernalia that go to make up the "new company town."

> Within the company's high walls, people laze on hammocks strung between pine trees. Others pump iron in the gym, practice jump shots on the gleaming basketball court, or hang around the putting green, horseshoe pit, or beach volleyball court. Cooks harvest oregano from the herb garden for the day's meal. Free bananas are everywhere. And an army of services—bookstore, dry cleaner, hairdresser, nail salon— complete the self-contained community. Notes thirty-year-old Christine Choi: "You never have to leave the place." (Useem 2000)

The head of human resources of the same company is quoted as saying: "It gives you a balanced life without having to leave."

Nevertheless, some people do want to leave and do not want to put in the normative 10-, 12-, or 14-hour days that such arrangements are designed to accommodate. Americans have begun to hear more about people who want to "scale back" (Ehrenreich 1995), about the need for family-friendly policies that allow people to reserve time for "care work" of various kinds, of the desire of some people to retire early rather than work long hours late in life. The people we talked with are among those who are exploring these options. For a variety of reasons—the desire to pursue personal dreams, to serve the community, to ease into retirement, or, most commonly, to spend time with young children—the people we met had another vision of professional technical work, one that allowed time for other things, time to put work in its place.

They are not alone. Penny Becker and Phyllis Moen (1999) found that the dual-career couples in their study wanted to work, on average, twelve fewer hours per week. Women with preschoolers wanted to work on average 25–28 hours per week, down from the 41–47 hours a week worked by the women with technical and professional jobs. The men worked even longer. Becker and Moen (1999) refer to the desire for less work time as "scaling back," implying that the experience of working long hours has caused some Americans to modify their view of work's place in their lives. Jerry Jacobs and Kathleen Gerson (1998, 2000) found a very similar pattern. Their analysis shows that professionals and managers are particularly likely to work long hours and to wish to reduce their work

time. Women tend to work shorter hours than men do, but, interestingly, men and women are equally likely to want to reduce their
work hours by roughly similar amounts. Moreover, Jacobs and Gerson conclude that the desire to reduce work hours is not confined to
the years when parents have young children at home. They suggest
that the motivations for wanting to reduce work hours are not uniform; on the contrary, they appear to vary among groups within the
population.

Why do many technical professionals want to reduce their work
hours? What do they want to do with the time freed up by working
less, and why do they want to do it? Is this something they have
wanted to do all along, or has it emerged from their experience of
working long hours? The answers they give suggest that at least
some technical professionals want to develop lives that do not re-
volve solely around paid employment. Unlike the people who
Hochschild describes in *The Time Bind*, they are not fleeing into the
workplace. Rather, they define a "life" as involving some combination of paid employment and other activities. What they want, and
why they want it, varies considerably.

What Else Is There Besides Work?

Prevailing cultural images make it hard for many Americans to
imagine engineers, computer scientists, or technical writers as anything other than full-time workers with lives dominated by their
jobs. They are commonly seen as one-dimensional types focused exclusively on their technical projects. When they are seen in a more
glamorous light, as highly paid professionals with good careers in
rapidly growing fields, this assumption makes one wonder why they
would want to cut back on the time they spend on work, and how it
would ever be possible for them to do so.

If there is one reason for cutting back that does have some cultural resonance, even for technical professionals, it is to raise a family; but this choice, of course, is "reasonable" only for women. Most
people can imagine that a mother, even a highly paid one, might
want to take some time off, or reduce her time at work, to look after
preschool children. Moreover, while most technical professionals
are still men, the minority of women in these fields is growing. It is

not surprising, then, that many of the people we talked with were mothers motivated to reduce their work hours by a desire to spend time with their children, or that their reasons for seeking to curtail their work schedules told the now familiar story of conflicts between the time demands of "greedy" professional careers and the desire to devote time to one's family. Such women have been at the forefront of most recent demands for reduced work time.

Many such women expressed feelings of being overwhelmed by all the work and responsibilities that they have to squeeze into a twenty-four-hour day. The demands generated by their children, their spouse, domestic work, and a full-time career are seen as simply too great to be juggled effectively. Susan, an engineer, clearly feels this way:

> Just the work load, the combination of the housework, the children, with working. I didn't think I could handle it all. And my husband, he's an attorney, so he doesn't work normal forty-hour weeks. He works sixty-hour weeks, and sometimes more. And a lot of the housework falls on me because he's out there working all the time. So it would just be too much to handle.

Corinne has come to a similar conclusion: "I had in my mind an idea that it would just be too much to try and juggle it all, especially working in the Loop. It's basically thirteen hours, you know, door to door, and, uh, to add on the time in the morning and the time at night, and the pick up and the drop off and the day care . . . I just didn't think it was viable."

The feeling of not having enough time to do everything is intensified by the fact that many women have time demands that are unpredictable. A technical emergency may keep them in the office longer than they expected, meetings may run late, a workaholic boss may want to chat even past normal work hours, and then there is the commute, which in midwestern winters can be notoriously unpredictable. All this is bad enough for the individual, but hours that are both long and uncontrollable present real problems for parents with responsibilities for child care (Negrey 1993).

Such problems can be solved, of course—as they have been by generations of career-oriented men in the past—by having someone else look after the children full-time. But most working mothers do not have a stay-at-home spouse to take on the job. Nor is this group financially able to support a full-time live-in nanny, and even if they could, few American parents, particularly in an era that emphasizes the importance of parental involvement with children, are comfortable with such an arrangement. A cleaning woman is often about as far as they are willing to stretch in the way of in-house service; a nanny would have smacked too much of an upper-class lifestyle. It is not for nothing that Robert Zussman (1985) called engineers, and by extension all technical professionals, "mechanics of the middle class." For some, family members provide support, but many have moved far from their homes of origin. For others the only alternative would be full-time day care.

Since the beginning of the feminist movement in the nineteenth century, collective day care has been the option proffered as the best arrangement to allow women with small children to take jobs. As the connotations of the term "collective day care" indicate, however, in the individualized culture of the United States this is not usually a popular option. Our respondents are no different in this respect, particularly in culturally conservative Cleveland. Many, like Corinne, are particularly opposed to large, organized day care facilities:

> But we did go and check out day cares, because I so much wanted to continue working. It was a change we weren't sure we wanted to make, and after about the fourth one my husband looked at me and said, "They remind me of an orphanage. These children are just a number." We checked up, the workers get paid minimum wage, they tend to change every three months, there's the sickness issue: it was not a situation we wanted our son to be raised in if we had a choice.

This is not a universal position among our respondents; a few had used or were using institutional day care on a part-time basis. But most of our respondents are uncomfortable with the idea of institutional day care, particularly if a child must be there five full days a week. In actuality, most of those who say they dislike this form of day care are not particularly familiar with it. Few cited any direct experience with centers or reported knowing of them from family or friends (at best, like Corinne, they had visited centers but had not made use of them). Their resistance to day care is not a function of bad experiences but instead is rooted in the general discomfort that day care arouses in many Americans. We heard lots of stories like Corinne's that emphasize the alleged regimentation and impersonality of day care centers.

Moreover, as we shall see in Chapter 6, the idea of full-time day care does not fit with our respondents' view that their involvement with their children benefits them as well as the children. It should be noted, however, that day care centers that the middle class can afford often differ little from our respondents' perception of them. Nor is there much likelihood that the kind of resources necessary to produce day care facilities of the kind that would be accepted by the American middle class—the kind universally available in France or Emilia-Romagna, for example—are likely to be available soon.

Family day care, the kind provided in someone's home, or occasionally by someone who comes to the house during the day, is more acceptable. Alice, an engineer who had actually helped establish a day care center at the research center where she worked, didn't use it herself: "I just couldn't put my daughter in organized day care," she said. Instead, she has chosen to have a "private sitter"—a neighbor who offers day care in her home. While this kind of care is more acceptable to most of the women we talked with, some still resist handing over care to relative strangers. Phyllis, a computer scientist, expresses this reluctance: "Well, I didn't like the ones I saw and I didn't like the idea of my son being raised by people that I didn't know at such a—being so young. And we went to a lot of places and—it felt very—it didn't feel right for us." Our respondents voiced particular concern about day care for young babies, and a more general concern about the very long hours that the children would have to spend in day care if it were available.

Often it is not. One engineer lives in a suburb of Chicago, not known for its social conservatism, where town regulations forbid the provision of day care before 7 A.M. This regulation makes day care inaccessible to her because she works long hours and has a lengthy commute.

This combination of wanting to spend time with one's children, the enormous time demands of work, and reluctance to make use of full-time day care has placed professional working mothers at the cutting edge of attempts to customize work time. Nonetheless, part-time technical professionals are a very diverse group. Even within the corporate world, but especially if one considers the experiences of self-employed contractors, the variety of part-timers covers a broad range. Not all of them are mothers, and their motivations for seeking part-time schedules are extraordinarily varied.

We found several who have reduced their work hours to pursue another activity from which they derive great pleasure. Catherine, an engineer with a large automotive company, is passionate about modern dance. The only way she can make the time for the long hours of practice that her dancing requires has been to work part-time. She is young and is not sure what the future holds, but she wants to give dancing a chance while she is still able. Working part-time as an engineer gives her the time to try out her avocation while still pursuing the career for which she trained.

Don, a young independent computer programmer in his late twenties, met us for coffee in downtown Chicago after a session of roller-blading along the Oak Street Beach front. He is making a lot of money as a top-rated Oracle programmer but has cut back on his consulting hours because he wants to devote more time to the recording studio he has built for use by local rock groups. Like the dancer, he enjoys technical work. It is not just a source of income, a glorified version of the waiting on tables done by actors to support their careers. Don wants to do more than just program, and the recording studio allows him to fulfill another dream.

Andrew, a forty-five-year-old engineer working in engine design for an automotive company, had been dissatisfied with his job when his company announced a program to provide flexible hours for some of its employees. He likes engineering, but he found his job a bit limiting. The flextime program was intended for subordinate employees, not engineers, but Andrew managed to persuade his employers to let him use it to pursue further education. For the past five years he has been studying to get his Ph.D. When we talked with him, he was close to finishing and was at the point of trying to decide what to do. He was torn between going back to his full-time job, combining part-time teaching with part-time engineering, and looking for a full-time teaching job (something he had grown more skeptical about while he was in graduate school). He seemed very unsure whether returning to full-time work of any sort was the answer. He liked working part-time, he said. "I've had such a good time doing it. When I worked full-time I was kind of miserable. . . .

I think I've been an easier person to live with for the past five years."

Others we talked with were more community-minded. Walt, an engineer in his late fifties, had been working part-time for more than a decade. He did not set out to work part-time; rather, he found corporate life uncomfortable and decided to work as a consultant. He found that he did not need to work full-time to support himself and his family, and he relished the ability to engage in other pursuits that a less than full-time schedule gave him. He told us that he had been very active in the environmental movement at one time, but that lately he had spent more of his time on volunteer engineering projects:

> My biggest thing lately is down at the [local public greenhouse]. I put in a misting system in three of their show houses, and I'm going to help put it in three more of them. There's nowhere else that I get referred to as a genius for the most simple-minded things such as making a shower or a spray system in a greenhouse. I really like working in greenhouses. That confined space, you engineer a space, and you engineer an environment for plants to grow. I did some work with a guy out in [a neighboring county] who had an organic vegetable-growing greenhouse, and put in a watering system for him one time. That ceased in the snow a few years ago. So I do work for [the local public greenhouse], and I take care of my church building. And right now I'm doing work at the [local nature center] on their project to dredge the [local ponds].

Walt speaks with evident enthusiasm about the pleasure he gets from doing even simple engineering tasks during his "time off." He deliberately avoids beating the bushes for additional paid engineering work so that he can do volunteer engineering in his expanded spare time.

Marjorie had not long been divorced when we met her. Before going back to devoting long hours to her business as an independent technical writer, she wanted to keep time free to join her environmentalist friends in prairie burning to emulate the traditional practices of the Native Americans who originally shaped the landscape. It is a way of maintaining contact with her friends as well as a way of helping the environment, but there is no way she could do it and work the long hours that she thinks a complete investment in building her business would take. Instead, she is content to do the small-scale jobs that come her way through her already established contacts and to worry about expansion later.

Jason, one of the few young men we interviewed, works part-time as a computer specialist at a local university and jealously protects his free time, as does his wife, a part-time nurse. They are both very active in their church and work on social justice issues. They have made a deliberate effort to work part-time to keep time free for this work; at least, they say, until they have children.

The cases of Walt, Marjorie, and Jason point to an important role for part-time workers: filling in the gap in community life created by the absence of those women who used to be available for volunteer work. If Robert Putnam is right and the family time squeeze is in part responsible for the decline in participation in a variety of community activities, then this kind of part-time work may provide one solution, if only for that segment of the middle class able to afford it.[1] Without falling into the trap of seeing volunteer work as a solution to all society's needs, we cannot doubt that in the absence of part-time workers with time to volunteer for community activities—time often given in the past by stay-at-home wives[2]—the long American tradition of such work would be in jeopardy.

At the other end of the age spectrum from Marjorie and Jason are those independent contractors—mostly men—who are using the reduction in their hours as a transition to retirement. Leonard, a programmer/analyst, retired from a large mining company after thirty years. He enjoyed the technical side of his job; indeed, he said that one of the attractions of retiring and going back to work part-time was that he was able to jettison his managerial responsibilities. But, as he puts it:

> After thirty years with the same company, I was ready for a change. There's always a debate about how big of a change. I wanted more

1. Putnam 2000 stresses that Americans are becoming more private and neglecting the public sphere in large part because of time pressures. See also Rifkin 1995 for a discussion of the role that volunteer work could play in improving the commonweal if paid work came to be reduced in importance.

2. See Daniels 1988 for an analysis of volunteer work traditionally done by upper-class women.

time off for myself. We also both have elderly parents. My parents live on their own. My father-in-law lives with us six months out of the year. Taking care of them was taking up a lot of time. I hadn't had a vacation in quite a while. That probably hastened my decision.

Caring for elderly parents is usually associated with the "sandwich generation," but in other respects Leonard shares with the other retired workers we met a desire to remain active in the technical work he enjoys while finding more time for travel, family, and leisure pursuits.

Since female technical workers were rare in the past, we were not surprised to encounter no older women who were bridging the gap to full retirement. We did meet a computer scientist, Karen, who had worked part-time as a nurse for many years while she was raising her children (one of whom had had significant health problems) and now has decided to continue to work part-time so that she can enjoy her family:

My family are all East, we have a home in the East. I want to be able to travel with my husband, which I wasn't able to do when the children were little. I want to be able to go and visit my children, and stay in our house where the kids can all visit easily because they're all within a reasonable radius of that particular house.

In effect, Karen is transitioning to retirement. She is reluctant to embark on a new, full-time career at age fifty because she wants to synchronize her life with the lives of her older spouse and adult children.

In short, to the large group of part-timers who seek reduced schedules to take care of small children we must add a wide range of individuals with a wide variety of motives. The modal part-timer is still the mother with small children, and most policies regarding part-time work are still constructed with these mothers in mind, but there are many others with different reasons for seeking to cut back on their time at work. Many of those we talked with, especially among the nonmothers, have reduced their work time as independent contractors. Because they have a marketable expertise that is in great demand, they can carve out for themselves a place where work time can be more manageable and flexible, or at least more under their own control. Clearly part-time work is much more diverse than is generally acknowledged. A significant number of people want to work part-time for reasons other than parenthood, and both organizational and national policies need to take these varying motivations into account.

Making the Decision

If there are many motivations for reducing time commitment at work, there are also multiple pathways to taking the plunge. Even the mothers of small children often discovered their need to work part-time in different ways. Once again, a rigid approach to part-time work does not fit the realities of part-time workers.

Many of the parents among our respondents had evolving, flexible views of their careers and work time. A few had planned all along to shift to part-time status when they had children, but more common are those who had not anticipated part-time work when they started out. A few had even explicitly decided *not* to cut back on their hours because of children. Beth, a part-time engineer for a chemical company, has four children. She has been working part-time since the second one (now ten years old) was about six months old, but she did not intend to work part-time when she began her family. In fact, she returned to full-time work after her first child was born and worked that way for almost two years. When her second child was born, she again returned to full-time work, but eventually she found that it was just too much:

> I guess I always thought that you have certain blocks of time during the day, that the second child would fit into the blocks with the first child, but it doesn't. I found that the first child took up x number of hours, and the second child took up an additional number of hours, and I had no time left to myself. That's why I decided to go part-time.

Beth seemed genuinely surprised that she had decided to cut back on her work hours. She had long thought that children could be fitted into her professional career without much difficulty. This surprise, which was not unusual, is perhaps understandable given the personal histories of many of those we interviewed. Technical women have had to fight hard to overcome the cultural prejudice against women in these fields. The struggle tends to weed out those who are unsure of their commitment. For many of these women, it is devoting time to family, not continuing working, that requires an explicit and sometimes difficult decision.

Their approach to part-time work has emerged from real experience, not from any decision taken early in life. They have revised their approach to work time as their lives have changed, supporting quite well Anita Garey's (1999) view that women approach work and family as a unified whole, not separate realms of experience. The process of revision, however, varies from woman to woman. Some women talk about a gradual discovery, as the birth of their child approached, that it would be too much to work full-time. More common is a reaction to the actual birth of the child. Many said they decided to work only part-time while they were on maternity leave. They described their part-time jobs as if they were an extension of their maternity leaves and talked about their unwillingness to go back to work so soon. Still others did not become part-timers until after the birth of their second or third child, finding that meeting the needs of several children made the time demands of their jobs unmanageable. A few (one man and several women) actually traded places with a spouse who worked part-time. Moreover, many redefined short-term part-time work into a more open-ended arrangement.

Maria, a computer scientist who worked as a part-time manager, decided after her child was born that "the balance wasn't right." She negotiated a trial part-time job as a manager of a group of professionals. This arrangement lasted for a year and a half, but she found that it demanded too many hours. Then she was approached by a woman who had transferred into her area and was seeking to share a job. The two worked out a shared management job and were able to sustain this partnership for four and a half years, until Maria's partner decided to take a leave. Unwilling to go back to full-time status, Maria searched for and found a new job-share partner (a man this time) and resumed work as a part-time manager.

Maria is unusual only in the complexity of her work history. We met many other technical professionals who find that their attitudes toward work time are evolving as they experience the reality of reduced work arrangements. Like Lucy, an automotive engineer, many find themselves wondering about options other than what they had planned in the first place:

> Who knows? I don't know what's going to happen three years from now. I might want to stay part-time for a very long time . . . as long as it's a challenging job for me. I might be happy with part-time for an extended period of time. Which I didn't think I would. It would be nice to be home, even if the kids were in school. To pick them up, just the peace of mind of being there. That would be nice for an extended period of time.

Lucy is not drifting away from work, as her emphasis on challenge makes clear. But she is exploring, in her own mind at least, changing her plans in ways she did not earlier anticipate. Cynthia Epstein and her colleagues (1999) found a similar kind of evolution among part-time lawyers, despite the more severe career consequences facing them.

This fluidity also characterizes the careers of the nonmothers we met. Catherine, the engineer who wants to dance, talks about her decision to work part-time in a way that makes it sound as if she almost backed into it:

> I was feeling a little harried. I had a number of things going on at the same time and I was really going out of my mind. I was dancing, which I always do, and working. And I had some other things going. I think I was taking a brush-up course at the same time, which was so much more than I had anticipated. I had also started doing volunteer work at a teenage crisis intervention center in town, which I was really enjoying, at least at first. It required quite a bit of time. So I guess, besides my personal chores or whatever I have to do, I also have other interests. So I went down to part-time. I was really going mad. It was a good thing, what I did. And then I decided to go back to school, so I just stayed part-time. And that worked out really well.

The process of experimentation and adaptation that Catherine describes was echoed by many technical professionals, both mothers and nonmothers. She makes clear that she is trying things out, without having a clear idea of what she wants; she also changed what she was doing as she discovered either that things didn't work (doing too many things at once) or that they did (going back to school, continuing to work part-time).

As we will see in Chapter 5, many contractors, particularly the men, did not become contractors with the intention to work part-time. They left the corporate world to achieve independence or to escape the rat race. They discovered that it was possible to work part-time and they decided that that was what they wanted. In some cases this decision resulted from a sudden confrontation with the possibility of burnout; in others it was a more gradual process of settling into a part-time work pattern that turned out to be comfortable for them.

Thus it is very difficult to predict which people will seek part-time schedules, under what circumstances, and for how long. The decision to become a part-time worker emerges from the experience of trying to integrate work and other aspects of one's life. It cannot be fitted easily into a standardized model.

Customizing Work Time

Just as there is no single motivation that explains all part-time workers' decisions, no single path to part-time work, the actual definition of part-time work and the kind of arrangements that make it possible vary from individual to individual. Indeed, we even encountered a few people who have been involved in more than one form of part-time work, though the choice was not always theirs. Even successful part-timers have had to negotiate their schedules with employers or customers, who can be less than accommodating.

One of the most obvious variations involves the distribution of work time: the number of hours worked and how those hours are distributed across the week or year. Part-time work is officially defined by the Bureau of Labor Statistics as work that occupies fewer than 35 hours a week, but many organizations have their own policies that define what part-time work is for them. Most of the people we interviewed accept the idea that part-time means fewer than 40 hours (although we did find a few people who define 40 hours as part-time, since their normal workweek could easily have been much longer). But we found that most part-time technical professionals define part-time in an individual way; they have worked out arrangements in accordance with what is possible and what they seek to gain by working part-time.

Some people define part-time as working less than a full day five days a week. This is often the choice of parents who have school-age children at home or who have access to day care that they find acceptable. Jim, for example, a divorced computer scientist who has custody of his two children, decided to seek work as a contractor because it allows him to work when he wants. He estimates that he works about 33 hours a week, often coming in late or going home early because of his children's needs (one is in school, the other in preschool). Barbara, a computer scientist employed by a telecommunications company, works 32 hours a week, five days a week. She started out working a three-day week, but found that her employer was pressuring her to work more hours. She increased to four days a week for two and a half years. After her second child was born, she decided to shift to a five-day schedule. "It was as if everything revolved around child care in my life and the best child care I could find was in a five-day-a-week program." Barbara also finds, however, that working five days a week has reduced the pressure on her to work more hours. Since she is there every day, her boss and her colleagues do not miss her. She seems pleased that "a lot of people don't even realize that I'm part-time." This new arrangement works well, making both her family life and her work life more satisfactory.

Another pattern for part-time workers is to work full days but fewer than five a week. Some share a job, working half a week while their partner covers the other half. Typically, this arrangement involves a three-day workweek, with some overlap to allow the partners to bring each other up to speed. Others have negotiated or developed part-week schedules on their own. Susan, an engineer for an automobile manufacturer, works 24 hours a week, three days a week. Her employer provided a series of options (20 hours, 24 hours, 30 hours), but Susan said that she wound up negotiating her own schedule once she had chosen the number of hours she wanted to work. Her schedule is a product of two factors. It fits well with the demands of her current project: some jobs require attending significant numbers of meetings but hers does not, so she is able to be away from work two days a week. It also works for her at home, since she is reluctant to put her children in full-time day care. She concluded that the three-day-a-week schedule made the most sense after she had her second child:

> It wasn't as hard with one, I thought. Because when I got home, she was the focus of my attention. But when there were two, I felt like that time between when I got home and the time when I had to put them to bed would be too short. And on top of that, it would be a little more chaotic, and I just thought that it would be unfair to the two of them.

Such patterns are typical of parents who have small or school-age children.

A few part-timers among the nonparents have worked out very different schedules consistent with the nonwork activities in which they are involved. Karen, for example, who reduced her hours so that she could travel with her husband and see her adult children, defines her schedule as part-time, but it is actually part-year. She works 80 percent of normal time, "and basically what it means is that I work more than forty hours a week when I'm in town and I'm able to take off ten or eleven weeks in a year. . . . The part-time is part of the year rather than part of the week or part of the day. And for me that works out really well."

Many retired workers also try to work intermittently, accepting work when it suits them to free up time for travel, hobbies, holidays, and the like. Even some younger contractors try to create gaps in their work years to pursue other activities. Tony, a forty-seven-year-old technical writer, talked about the kinds of things he likes to do with the time he has created for himself as a contractor: "Leisure is very important. I like to spend time with the Scouts. I take my kids out hiking on two or three week-long trips each year. I like to take time off for vacations, to go to the shore, take Christmas off." Tony and some of the other part-timers we met did not mind working full-time when they were working, but they wanted blocks of time off during the year to accommodate activities that required travel or their undivided attention.

As we will see, variations in part-time arrangements are not confined to the actual schedules people work. Some find it attractive to combine part-time work with homework to facilitate child care or other domestic arrangements. Others consider such an arrangement anathema; they hate the isolation that goes with homework. Some have opted for contracting either because they want to or because they have to. They find that the independence it provides makes it easier for them to manage their time and find satisfying work. Others reject contracting, concluding that it is simply too difficult to manage the flow of work.

Obviously there is no single pattern that works for all part-timers. Each has her or his own needs, and each has tried to work out a schedule that meets them. Moreover, since people's attitudes toward part-time work change as their lives develop, it is not uncommon for them to try out more than one schedule. Effectively, the people we met are trying to customize their work hours. Choosing from a menu of preset options is not the ideal to which they aspire. Rather, they want to develop schedules that uniquely fit them. Despite the rigidity of most formal policies, many part-timers have been able to work out their own idiosyncratic arrangements.

Customizing a Life

We were surprised and impressed by the range of people who describe themselves as part-time workers and by the variety of stories they told us about their reasons for seeking part-time work, about how they came to a decision to seek part-time work, and about what worked for them. Despite the diversity of part-time workers, however, we also see a unifying element behind this variety of motivations and experiences. Our respondents are all, as we heard from them many times, trying to put work in its place; trying to blend paid employment with other activities. All of them have made a choice to live according to rules that differ from those prescribed by the organization's time schedule because of the pleasure they derive from other activities. What those other activities are varies; and what precisely they want from work varies as well. For all the people we talked with, a life includes work, but cannot and should not be reduced to it.

3

A Professional and More

Catherine wants to dance, Don wants to record rock and roll. Are they just slackers who want to mess around rather than buckle down to their "real" careers? Jason wants to spend time working for social justice when he is not working for his university's information technology department. Is he just a wishy-washy liberal hangover from the 1960s? Leonard and Michael are easing into retirement. Are they signs of a declining American work ethic just because they do not want to work full-time until they die? Hardly, and yet this is the way the discussion of work time is sometimes framed. Being serious about one's work is supposed to mean a full-time, indeed an extended time, commitment: every day, every week, for a lifetime. This is what is traditionally meant by having a "career." Anything less and work becomes just a job: something that pays the bills, easily put on and taken off, a way to pay for a life rather than part of life itself.

This perception is based on a view of work, shared by many on all sides of the sociopolitical spectrum, that sees professional and corporate careers as "greedy institutions" (Coser 1974). Working in a traditional profession is said to require nothing less than a round-the-clock commitment to the needs of the client and the pursuit of professional learning. Pursuing an organizational career is seen as requiring an equal dedication to meeting the organization's demands and climbing the bureaucratic ladder. To give up this kind of career in favor of "just a job" is portrayed as giving up any possibility of intrinsically interesting work, the kind of work that would reward an extensive education and a lifetime of attention. Careers, not jobs, are what help shape identities, give form to a work life, and gain public recognition for one's efforts.

All our respondents resist this view of work. Those easing toward retirement have had to convince both their employers and their families that they haven't given up on work "just yet." Those with avocations have to insist that they are not dilettantes, but are serious about their jobs. Professional women with children, in particular, have to resist the assumption that they have settled for the mommy track, a less demanding form of work, not really a career, just a job (although the man or woman in the next cubicle or office may be doing similar work but be on the fast track to the top).

Working mothers face an additional problem: a cultural view of the family as an institution as greedy and identity-determining as a career. Cultural norms of intensive mothering portray middle-class children as needing full-time personal care and interaction.[1] When they are young, it is argued, they need to bond with their mothers; when they are older, moms need to provide support for homework, music lessons, classes for the gifted, and, of course, the inescapable soccer. And if child rearing isn't demanding enough, Martha Stewart, on the road to becoming one of the most successful entrepreneurs of the decade, proclaimed that "people are trying, once again, to set a standard that'll be more conducive to raising good children and maintaining a nice house" (Holcombe 1998:43).

If the proliferation of elaborate cooking and decorating magazines and TV shows (including, of course, Martha's own empire) is anything to go by, the culture is saturated with a view of domesticity that would require not just a full-time housewife but full-time servants. The media have been full of images of successful women professionals returning home to cook dinner for their husbands as well as rescue their children from the supposed horrors of institu-

---

1. The children of the poor, on the other hand, are usually portrayed as not needing intensive mothering. To the contrary, they need a mom who works. For a discussion of the norms of intensive mothering, see Hays 1996.

tional child care.[2] No wonder working mothers have felt pressured for time.

Is it true that part-timers are not committed to paid employment, that they view it as a job rather than a "career"? Certainly many researchers have suggested as much. Carol Hakim (1993), for example, argues that part-time workers (most of whom are women) are less committed to work, make fewer investments in human capital as a result, and are more likely to have traditional attitudes toward gender roles (and be married to men with analogous attitudes) than full-time women workers. Even Anita Garey (1999), who is certainly more sympathetic to working women than Hakim, notes that the health care workers in her study rejected the idea of having careers because they implied an overwhelming commitment to work. Instead of being "career women," they had jobs they could keep in their place. It is always a mistake, however, to assume intent or commitment from observations of behavior alone (Becker 1960, Bielby and Bielby 1988, Moen 1985), and our professionals certainly had a different attitude toward work than Garey's health care workers. All of them see themselves as committed to having careers, just not the same careers their fathers might have had. It is only by assuming that an unbounded commitment to paid employment is synonymous with "career" that one could construe our respondents as uncommitted.[3]

The mothers among our respondents certainly see themselves as moms, even soccer moms, but motherhood does not have the same meaning for them as it did to their own mothers. Their view of motherhood involves an implicit challenge to the view that it, too, is a greedy institution that makes unlimited demands and therefore makes a career impossible. To the technical professionals we met, motherhood is a source of pleasure, a role one chooses, not an unlimited obligation. They talk about it in terms similar to the way all of our respondents talk about work and similar to the way non-

2. One of us was asked by a local newspaper to comment on this "phenomenon." Despite the lack of evidence that anything of the sort is occurring, the writer's editor had apparently concluded, on the basis of his own experience, that this was a major national trend.

3. Joan Williams (2000) makes a similar argument in suggesting that the "ideal worker norm," which assumes that work means full-time, unchallenged commitment, is not the only form of work commitment that is possible.

mothers discuss their activities away from work. Both mothers and nonmothers want to put work in its place. Both want to enter freely into both work and nonwork activities without letting either consume all of their time and being.

Forging a New Identity: Being a Professional

Virtually all of our respondents—women and men—like to work and say so. They have jobs they enjoy and in which they find considerable gratification. Holly, an engineer, exclaims, "It's great, it's wonderful, it's very gratifying to have a career, and especially when it's something you love doing, that you spend your life working toward. I've never had any doubts that this is what I love doing." Another engineer, Nancy, can't imagine quitting: "That's scary to me, not to be able to work. I don't work because I have to for the money. I work because I enjoy it. Oh, boy, to think of giving it up!"

Technical work for the people we met is a source of intense joy and satisfaction. They have not drifted into it for want of a better alternative. They do not do it just because it pays the bills. They do not equate organizational success with career satisfaction. It is the work, the design, the programs, the problem-solving, or the writing to which they refer. One can see it not just in their words but also in the visible enthusiasm with which they say them.

Being a technical professional is part of their identity. None of them has stopped thinking of herself as an engineer, computer professional, or technical writer. Many tell stories of having chosen technical work early in their childhood and of pursuing it consistently since then. As Linda, an environmental engineer, put it: "Of course I'm an engineer, after all that investment in my education, and it's what I do." Technical work of one kind or another *is* what they do, and the hours they work do nothing to change that.

Moreover, most of our respondents value their work because it is *technical* work. They like the challenges presented by technical problems and they like the diverse problems they encounter and the feeling of accomplishment that their work gives them. Tina, an engineer who is part of a job-share, actually changed jobs within her company (a very difficult thing to do as a part-timer) in order to obtain work that is more challenging:

I really want to learn more technically. Like right now, I'm really interested in new software development paradigms and how to apply them. And that's what I really like about this job: we have a brand-new project, and we're responsible for software development and the process, figuring out what the process ought to be. And I really want to become an expert in that.

Carl, a retired engineer working as a consultant, conveys a similar sense of enthusiasm about the technical side of his work. He told us that he has no plans to retire completely (although he is in his late seventies) and talked excitedly about what he sees as the increased technical challenges he has encountered as a consultant:

I get access to other people's technology, which I can't tell anybody, but my fund of knowledge has increased a great deal since I became a consultant. I could read literature before, but it would be difficult to tell what was something they *might* do and what was something they were actually doing. After I've been working for a little while, I have a much better grasp of what's really there. It just makes you, if anything, a better expert.

This is an aspect of the technical mentality—the professional orientation, if you like—that employers try to exploit when they offer potential new recruits new "toys" to play with.

One of the ways this professional orientation plays out is in the pride people take in their work. Gideon Kunda (1992) has noted how this culture plays a role in encouraging hard work in many engineering organizations, and it is not restricted to full-time employees. Part-time professionals frequently claim they are able to accomplish almost as much as part-timers as they had done as full-timers. In fact, many indicate that they feel they have a responsibility to work hard *because* they are part-timers. Barbara, the computer scientist, recognizing that she often works longer than the hours she is being paid for, notes, "I guess it's probably more me than anything. Because you know, I want to pull my own weight, so it's probably me putting pressure on myself more than my employer." Holly recalled her surprise and disapproval when she discovered how much time she had wasted when she was working full-time:

When you're full-time, you have no concept of the value of time. People stand around shooting the breeze, they put in more hours, but they're down in the cafeteria talking with the boys until eight-thirty and take an hour and a half for lunch. They work until six, but half that time is . . . I'm very "Let's go, let's go, I have five minutes, let's get it done." I don't stand around and shoot the breeze, hardly ever. Maybe twice in the last year have I gone with anybody to lunch. You're just more aware of the value of time.

From some perspectives, such conscientiousness could look like exploitation, and perhaps in a strict sense it is, but it is also the result of a professional identification with a job well done.

Cindy, a computer professional in her late thirties with two children, feels that her experience as a full-time worker helps her productivity as a part-time worker. She says:

I think that if a person really makes an effort to get involved and not let themselves get sidetracked, they can do as much as the people who are working full-time. And I think also that it helped that I had a lot of experience before I even went part-time, so that helped a lot. Because I don't think anybody could tell that, by the amount of work I did, they couldn't tell.

Although she thinks her full-time record helped build her reputation as a reliable worker, she has maintained her productivity while cutting back her hours.

We heard many stories from part-timers who claim that their colleagues are unaware that they do not work full-time because they get the job done, or who boast that their productivity surpasses that of their full-time counterparts. There is a strong sense among them that they are fully equal to the full-timers, still valuable workers who can get the job done. Barbara's statement to the effect that she has a professional obligation to do the job—to "pull her weight"—is a common refrain, something we heard repeatedly from salaried employees and contractors alike.

The important point here is not that part-time workers are more productive, though there is evidence that they are,[4] but that they strongly identify with their work. While their protestations of supe-

4. For a review of the evidence about productivity, see Williams 2000: 96–101nn.

rior productivity reflect a certain defensiveness, an affirmation to themselves of their seriousness as workers, they also directly reflect their professional commitment. They see doing a good job as a professional obligation because they remain identified with their professions. Part-time they may be, but this does not, at least in their own eyes, make them any less an engineer, technical writer, or computer professional.

Maintaining their professional commitment is an important reason that many of the mothers have continued working as part-timers rather than staying home full-time. Danielle is typical: "I don't want to be a full-time mom. Not that full-time motherhood isn't a great thing. It's just that I spent five years getting a degree and eight years building a career. I just can't let go just like that, and I don't want to. When my kids are back in school, I want to still have a career."

Many of the engineers and computer professionals decided to go into technical work in high school, and because both occupations are relatively unusual for women, the choices were very conscious and deliberate. Staying on track through undergraduate programs that are not always friendly to women also required strong commitment. Technical work, for women in particular, is a vocation, something they strongly identify with.

Some, like Barbara, the computer scientist, are concerned that a prolonged absence from the workplace will lead to technical obsolescence: "Well, in this field, the technology just moves so fast. In order to keep up, you just have to be there. And when I look at the technology, what it was five years ago and what it is now, it's just tremendous, you just have to stay in it if you want to keep up." Keeping up is not merely an obligation, it is a thrill, and it is part of the joy of work.

Not all of the people we met, of course, are so excited about their work. Some admit that they are less fanatical in their commitment to work than they used to be, that they are no longer so willing to work constantly, to bring work home, and to drop everything in order to complete work tasks. Nonetheless, they still value work highly. Most of them, after all, have made an explicit decision to continue to work rather than to quit precisely because they cannot imagine not working at all. Tina, an engineer, put it this way:

> Being part-time, you travel in the circles with the moms who don't work outside the home. I set up a play group on one of my days off, so

I get to know all these moms, and I realize how important work is to me and how much I enjoy it. Because when I spend time with them, they do not have that other aspect to their lives.

Maria, a computer scientist, expresses similar sentiments:

My friends from college that I've known the longest, those that don't work, it's the typical "I don't know how you do it" kind of thing. At various points, when I'm part-time, I've said, "Oh it would be nice to be off all the time." But then my sanity check comes in and says, "You like what you do." And others say, "You've just got the ideal," which I believe I do.

Maria claims that she is actually a better worker now. Whereas before, as a full-timer, she felt that she was neither a good worker nor a good mom, now she has the chance to be both in a way with which she is comfortable. Wendy makes it clear that Maria is not alone in the sentiment: "I think being an engineer is part of me and so is being a mother, and to say which one is higher, I think they're a package deal."

And it is not simply the mothers who express a desire to be more than one thing. Tony, a successful consultant–technical writer who consciously limited his hours to 30 a week, sounds very much like Maria when he says: "I enjoy what I do; I get a sense of satisfaction in doing good user manuals. But that's only part of me. I want to grow the other part."

The pleasure that part-time technical professionals take in their work comes out clearly when they talk about the financial consequences of working part-time. Virtually all the people we met, whatever the reason they had decided on part-time work, had paid a financial price for the decision. Yet we heard no suggestion that they saw their paid employment as less important than their full-time work had been, as something they cared less about because it brought in less income. On the contrary, they emphasize that they work for rewards other than money, pointing to the satisfactions of the work they are doing.

Retired professionals frequently talked about the unimportance of the monetary rewards their work brought them. Wendell had begun teaching part-time twenty-five years ago, while he was still employed full-time as an electrical engineer, and he went right on teaching after he retired. "It wasn't just about money," he said. "The money was sort of an incentive. I just liked the idea. It's just a matter of an interest, not that I expected to make a lot of money out of it." Many other part-timers echo these sentiments. Martin, a computer professional working as a contractor, confesses that since he's been working reduced hours, money has become less important to him. He doesn't believe he has suffered much economically, but he doesn't seem to care, either: "I can't say the money's been any less, but frankly, things like being of use to other people have been of greater importance than actually getting monetary reward from it. Although they tend to go together in data processing nicely." Part-time technical professionals, whether or not they are financially motivated, consistently emphasize the pleasure and satisfaction they get from actually doing technical work.

Nonetheless, most of the people we talked with are practitioners, not managers (Evetts 1996). They write the code, prepare the manuscripts, deal with the customers, and solve problems. Only a few directly supervise others. This finding might be taken as evidence that they have chosen jobs rather than careers, that they are less committed to excelling in an occupation when to do so would require them to climb the ladder to higher management.

It is certainly true that some of our younger respondents believe their choice to work part-time has either delayed or eliminated their opportunities for career advancement. Tina, an engineer-manager, talks about some of the negative consequences of her job-share: "The cons are that if you're interested in moving up, you're not going to move as fast. You can't put as much effort into your career as you did before." When we asked whether she had come to terms with this situation, however, she said: "Yeah. 'Cause you gain so much more. I don't feel like I really lost anything. I just gained a lot more."

Paula, a very successful engineer in her early thirties, says, "I'm not interested in getting promoted. I'm more interested in becoming a technical expert. And developing a lot more technical expertise in software development. So I think I kind of really pushed for this job. Because I knew I could do that." Expertise in software development defines her ambitions in the profession, and she feels she would lose it as a manager. When she thinks about her career, she thinks about broadening her technical expertise rather than getting promotions. As a technical worker, she does the actual work instead of managing the budget. Besides her wish to remain technical, she views management as a hassle. She has not been trained in management and does not want to do it enough to spend extra time at work. By working part-time, she stays technical and claims her identity as an engineer.

Philip, an engineer who has chosen to work for a smaller company, in part because it allows him to limit his hours, says much the same thing:

> I don't want to move up into management. One thing I saw down at [large electronics company], if you do well, their idea of rewarding you is moving you up into management. That's not where I want to be, and in fact, the people that do not want to do that tend to get pushed off into the corner, instead of just being left to do their job. I'm happy with what I'm doing. Basically, the whole target of my career is helping people use technology. And that's all I really want to do is to get the technology in the hands of the people in ways that help them.

Both Philip and Paula limit their hours deliberately and consciously eschew the management track, but they can hardly be described as uncommitted to their work.

Even those who do think they have made a sacrifice in giving up a chance at promotion reconcile themselves to it in a way not possible for someone who has traded a good job for a boring, routinized one, or for whom climbing the corporate ladder is the primary goal. Gwyn, a senior technical programmer, sums up the opinions of many part-timers:

> I bucked the code. There's so much pressure to keep going after the American Dream. I think [working part-time] kind of helped because it's a double-edged sword. They don't want you to keep moving up because if you're part-time they don't think you can handle it. So I get to stay and do what I want to do. I guess that's the choice I've had, saying how far I want to go right now. Count me out for moving up, but this is where I want to be.

This is a common response of technical professionals in any setting. Many technical specialists are simply more interested in technical work than in pursuing managerial ambitions. We found similar responses in a high-powered British R&D lab years ago from young engineers totally engrossed in the technical aspects of their work (Whalley 1986).

The attitude of technical professionals toward promotion has always been complex. Many express ambivalence about a fast-track career because it would lead them out of technical work into management. Leonard, a retired engineer, talks about how much he prefers his current work as a contractor to his old job; he doesn't want "to run projects, to fight with management." He once had a management job, but confesses, "I was happiest when I got out of it." Others are reluctant to accept the time demands that sometimes go along with higher levels of responsibility. A few, however, do want to be promoted to management. Harriet, who has had several stints of part-time work, confesses that she has rediscovered her desire for a career. "When I was in the prior position, I pretty much gave up all ambition, and I've decided now that was a very foolish thing to do. Now I've made it clear to my boss that I do want to be back on the career track." She sees her management chain as "extremely liberal minded," and even feels that "there's some hope now" that she may be given managerial responsibility without having to abandon her part-time schedule.

Note that part-timers who want managerial positions and those who want only to continue with technical practice talk about their professional identities and their commitment in the same way. There is no sense that those who want management positions are in any way more identified with their work than those who are content to remain practitioners. Technical professionals' ambivalence toward promotion to management is no indication of lack of commitment to their work. Indeed, studies have found that it is the most technically involved and technically committed of professionals who are the least interested in management (McIlwee and Robinson 1992, Whalley 1986).

If a career implies a commitment to the corporate ladder, then most of our interviewees have jobs, living very much in the present and seeing their work as a part of life, not the whole of it. Yet "job" is a far too limited word to capture these people's orientation to work. They are committed professionals, committed if not to their company, then at least to their skills and their occupations. In some ways, their orientation is closer to that of the traditional craft-worker than to that of the corporate professional. They want to re-design what is meant by having a career, to strip it of its necessary assumptions of greedy time demands and organizational ladder climbing. For them having a career means being committed to one's expertise, whether within a corporation or outside of one. They do not want mere jobs, uninteresting work done simply for the pay. They want and have involving, interesting work, around whose time demands they choose to set distinct boundaries. They identify with their profession. They talk about having a career. They simply do not accept that a career has to be pursued the old way, that a profession or career has to be all-absorbing.

Forging a New Identity: Being a Mom

If all our part-timers have to redefine what having a career means so that it fits their chosen work strategy, the working mothers have the additional task of reconstructing the image of domesticity. As we will see in Chapter 6, most are unhappy with what Joan Williams has called the "full commodification" model—paying to have someone look after children full-time and do all the house-work—at least when it comes to institutionalized day care (Williams 2000:40). Neither, however, do they buy into a cultural package of domesticity that would put women back in the home in a replay of the 1950s. They certainly do not identify themselves as housewives or even as homemakers.

Perhaps the most important thing about the way these women talk about their family life is what is *not* mentioned. No one talks about a desire to cook elaborate or nutritious meals. Certainly no one talks about a desire to clean house, or even to pursue the de-lights of decorating. These women do not work part-time so they can have the martini ready for their husband as he returns from a long day at the office. They do not feel the need to be home while their husband travels. They do not mention the need to provide a warm and comforting home environment as a haven in a heartless world. These are women who, at least until they had children, saw themselves as pursuing a career of equal value to their husbands'. Nor do they typically use the language of "caring for" or "looking after" that has come to symbolize the feminine substitute for the masculine talk of "making money" or "being a success." In Joan Williams's language again, the women we talked with are more like "tomboys" than "femmes" (Williams 2000:181), perhaps unsurprisingly, given the types of careers they have chosen.

What they do talk about is their identity as moms and wanting to spend time with their children. If work can be enjoyable and satisfying and a source of positive self-imagery, so can child rearing. Though we found a real dislike of institutionalized day care, the response to other forms of child care is almost invariably cast in the positive language of enjoying being with their children rather than saving them from less desirable alternatives. Some would argue that this resistance to full-time day care is an example of traditionalism, and perhaps in some ways it is. As Williams points out, however, this attitude is widespread in the United States, lacking as it does either an aristocratic tradition of delegated child rearing or a socialist history of collective child care. Before we can ascribe our respondents' attitudes to a return to a prefeminist traditionalism, however, we need to look more closely.

The prime reason for changing their work arrangements was undoubtedly the desire to spend time with their children. As Julia, a contractor–technical writer, puts it: "If you're not going to stay home with them, why have them?" Given this desire, many, like Wendy, are unhappy with the prospect of working full-time and rushing through their lives, giving only cursory attention to their children: "I'd say that even before I got pregnant, I realized that I'd be getting home at seven at night, or six-thirty— Well, if the kids go to sleep at eight . . . I put two and two together and figured that I'd only be able to spend an hour or two with my kids, and I just wasn't happy with that." In this case, day care would be no solution to the desire to spend time with children. Children and adults just function on different clocks.

For others, such as Danielle, the issue is finding time to be with the children after the household chores are done:

> Well, I wouldn't have enough time with my child. I would just be running through life every day, just trying to get everything done that needs to be done, and I'm not really enjoying myself. From what I've seen of people and friends that I've talked to, you can go part-time with a small

child, but if you're full-time you get up in the morning, dash off to day care, go to work, come home, do all the things, get through the day. You really don't have much of a family life or time with your children.

If time with children is valued, then space needs to be made for it in a busy day.

Time spent with children is valued and not to be rushed. It should not feel like work in the negative sense of the word. Many mothers express concern over their state of mind after returning from eight, nine, or ten hours in an office. Nancy, who is employed as a part-time engineer and works much of her time at home, feels that a full-time career is simply incompatible with her view of what time with her family should be like:

> We would come home in the evening after working—we would work ten-hour days and enjoyed working. I'd go over and he wasn't quite done so I'd go back and start working and he'd come back and I wasn't done—we came home tired and mentally spent, and we didn't know how we would fit a child into that. You're coming home with no energy left, but yet a child who has been left all day is now demanding your attention. So one of our extreme considerations is that we'd have to have some time for this child that was fun—that he was part of our life. You know, we do laundry one night, we go shopping, we do bills, and we found that the time was already taken—where do you fit the baby in? So that was another significant consideration to us—we don't want to be burned out. Let's get him in bed as fast as we can. We want to crash.

Reducing hours at work not only allows more time to be with the children but it saves the parents from being burned out by long work hours with the chores still left to be done. As interviews with children have suggested, having less stressed parents who can give them their full attention is even more important to children than increasing the amount of time together (Galinsky 1999).

For some, it is simply a matter of having the ability to sit down and enjoy an unhurried, relaxing moment as nothing more than a regular mom. Again Nancy:

> Every day I set aside an hour that's his time. Whatever he wants to do—whether that's Play-doh or coloring or stacking blocks—and I

find that's critical because otherwise, even though I'm home, he wouldn't experience quality time. Usually the mornings were sort of our time to get things done around the house or do errands and stuff like that. And then the afternoons were our time to have fun together. So if I had to go out and do something, I would do that and get that done, and then I would always make time for fun.

This kind of individual attention is difficult to provide after a busy day and a long commute.

There is little talk here of "sacrificing for the children" or about children's need for "intensive mothering" (Hays 1996). Even when children's needs are mentioned, the talk soon turns to the wishes of the parent as well. Susan puts it this way: "I just felt they needed me more. Working forty or sixty hours a week and traveling and such, I didn't want to miss out on them and I didn't want them to miss out on me either."

Another engineer, Sarah, adds:

Some mothers I don't think feel the same way that I do. I have a cousin who has three kids as well and she puts her kids into day care and she doesn't have a problem with it. Well, it really bothers me when I'm not there. Even now. Just getting home from work—not that they are not being well taken care of, because I know they are— it's just more that I would like to be there experiencing the kids and have more time to spend with them on their schoolwork or working on their projects with them, taking them to classes. . . .

These are not parents who talk about sacrificing their own time to schedule elaborately their children's lives—though some do just that.

Nor do they talk about the child's need for extended and close interaction with their parents. Instead, they talk about their valuing this time for their own enjoyment and sense of accomplishment. For them, parenting is more than just a job they need to do. They want to partake fully of their parenting experience, and at the same time simply to have fun playing with their children. Donna, for example, emphasizes her own needs: "I feel like I want to be there when they come home. I don't know what's best for them, I'm guessing what's best for them is for me to be home, but most of this is my need. Most of this is for my own reasons."

Barbara's perspective is very similar: "I think part of it was self-ish, I want that time with the kids. The opportunity to work for a living is always going to be there, but the opportunity to spend time with your children is not."

For most of these professionals, child care is a fulfilling vocation. In that respect, it is much like their technical profession.

The desire to spend more time with their children came as a surprise to some of the women we met. If they thought about family at all while they were building their careers, they assumed they would "fit it in." These, after all, are women who committed themselves to nontraditional occupations at an early age, or whose own mothers were employed. For example:

> My mom always worked since I was about three years old, so I've always seen her work full-time, and as a child growing up that is what I saw and I didn't think that I would have problems with it. After my first child, I thought, "Three months and I'll go back to work." But my feelings changed after I had a child. Maternal feelings come out, I suppose. I don't know. I just wanted to spend more time with them.

All of the women had grown up in environments that encouraged them to pursue their careers. Many had faced an educational and work environment where they had had to assert vigorously that they were "just as good as the men." It is not surprising that many had not thought through their family and career plans.

In the 1990s, they were not alone. Anna Quindlen (1995), after noting that she had been heavily criticized for giving up her demanding position as a *New York Times* columnist for the more flexible work of writing fiction, recognized that she, too, had been surprised by her response to having children. She had been totally uninterested in having children during her twenties as she built up her career, but "my children were indeed behind this decision, as they have been behind literally every decision about the broad parameters of my life I have made since the eldest was born a dozen years ago. They have given me perspective on the pursuit of joy and the passage of time."

Women have had to fight hard to resist the assumption that all women should want in life is a home and children, and, as Betty Holcombe's (1998) review of the literature suggests, the battle is not over. Many professional women who came of childbearing age in the 1990s, however, find themselves in a different situation. Having established themselves as career women, some find themselves surprised by the pleasures and satisfactions that child rearing can offer.

Nonetheless, this is still a gendered preference. We found few men who had chosen to reduce work time to spend more time with their children. And those who did were often in unusual circumstances—single fathers with custody of their children, for example. But in that case, is staying home with children really a choice at all for most women, since social factors all but compel women to be the caregivers (Beechey and Perkins 1987)? The observations of the women we talked with suggest that it is. Insofar as humans can make a free choice at all, these women have done so. We do not challenge the role of the prevailing social mores, but our respondents insist that their decision to look after the children is a voluntary one. There is no talk of "feeling a need" or of "having to" look after the children. Some even recalled discussions about the possibility of their husband's staying home instead; but it rarely seemed like a difficult decision because of their own desire to assume the child care. Danielle recalls: "I said something to him like 'Well, maybe I'll go back full-time and you stay home part-time.' And he said OK. And I was like 'Oh, no, I didn't really mean it.'" We asked: "Why not?" "Because I enjoyed my two days with my son."

While the structural consequences of such choices may be to free men to devote more time to work (Williams 2000), when respondents talk in this way it is hard to justify the claim that this choice simply reflects a gendered ideology of domesticity that pushes women into the home. At least the force of that ideology seem to be no more irresistible than that of the ideology of work or of feminism, which reputedly is pushing them into the workplace. These women argue that spending time with children is a positive attraction, desirable on its own terms. Like all work, children can at times be burdensome. Nevertheless, they can also be fundamentally rewarding, especially if one has the means to devote time to them without their becoming the defining feature of one's existence.

In a few cases—particularly in more traditional Cleveland—the option of having the husband stay home to look after the children is rejected on the traditional grounds that child care is woman's work.

But, as Nancy's account makes clear, even these seemingly traditional choices are often more complex than they may first seem:

> My husband and I, when we had gotten married, had discussed that
> one of us would stay home if we had a child, so it was kind of like
> "hmmm . . ." Actually they extended the part-time option to both
> my husband and me. For a while we thought he was going to take it,
> because I was up for promotion to director. And then we weren't—
> being Christian, we just really didn't have a sense of peace about that,
> so we switched to me staying home, and that was the right answer.

This is a clear example of a traditional ideology—in this case reli-
gious—overcoming other factors; it is distinctive, however, in being
so unusual.

In other instances, such as Maria's, women feel it is easier for
them to ask for part-time work than it is for their husbands: "He
would be open to that, he likes to stay home with the kids, but I
don't think there was an opportunity for him, for his type of job.
Plus being a man, I don't think his firm would give him the opportunity to do that." There is certainly evidence that men find it
harder than women to ask for and be granted part-time positions. At
the same time, as in this case, people often assume as a matter of
cultural perception that employers will say no to men; certainly, in
the absence of cultural support for fathers' staying home, men are
less likely to ask for part-time schedules than are women, for whom
it is culturally normal.

The suggestion that there was a real alternative of the husband
staying at home may simply be a token offered up to an ideology of
gender equality, but it is interesting that it is made at all. It is doubt-
ful that a sample of technical professionals even ten years ago would
have suggested this possibility. Evidence is growing, moreover, that
young fathers are increasingly willing to reduce their work hours to
spend more time with their children (Coltrane 1996), and while
some of the women we talked with have spouses who were reluctant to consider this option, their wives often pitied rather than re-
sented them. "I don't think he really knows what he is missing. I'm
not saying he doesn't enjoy their company, he does. But I don't think
he has the free time just to be with them, and play with them, and
take care of them. I think men miss out on a lot of that. I think if he

was home with them more, he would enjoy it. But it's hard for men." Perhaps rather than talk only about the pressure on women to look after the children, it would be better to focus on the impact of patriarchy in denying men the opportunity to get the pleasure out of being with children that these women do.

Barbara Ehrenreich (1995), after noting that she had once cringed when friends cut back on high-pressure jobs to spend time with their children, fearing they were setting back women's progress in the workplace, argues that "women aren't downsizing in greater numbers than men simply because women tend to have a greater responsibility for children, but because child-raising provides us with a built-in standard for meaningful work." Unfortunately, it has often proved difficult to detach discussions of the pleasures of child rearing from the domestic package with which it has become entangled. Just as identification with meaningful work has come to be wrapped up in a male-oriented package with excessive demands on time within an organizational structure, so identification with bringing up children has come to be wrapped up in a female-oriented package that includes full-time homemaking. The women we talked with rejected both packages and were trying to forge something new. As Donna notes: "Staying home full-time, by the time he'd get home, I'd be going crazy. I have a lot better balance with part-time. There are some mothers that are perfectly comfortable with staying home and can handle it. Maybe it's because I had this experience before, of being in the workforce, that I enjoy it."

It is not just the words. When these women talk about their children they exhibit the same kind of excitement and positive delight as they do about the joys of technical work. Raising children is work, but it is enjoyable, satisfying work, and so is their job, as Phyllis makes clear: "The days that I'm home, I'm always glad to be home for the day. But I'm always glad to go to work, because if I had too much of one or the other, I don't think I would enjoy it. So this works out good for me."

These women refused to make the hard choice that conventional wisdom insists they must. They insist they are technical professionals *and* moms. If they spend less time in either role than tradition dictates, they are more than comfortable with their choice. "It is ideal," as more than one woman put it. The language they use about parenting is important. There is little talk of the children's "needs" or of "having to be there." Instead, they talk of "enjoyment," "satisfaction," and "interest." There is a remarkable similarity between the way they talk about their work as moms and their talk about their work as technical specialists.

Putting It All Together

These mothers are redefining what it means to be a successful technical professional. In effect, they are not only rejecting what Hochschild (1997) calls "the male world of work," with its stress on exclusive and unbounded commitment to the workplace, but also the "female world of unbridled domesticity." Rather than "making sacrifices," they speak of opportunities, of feeling lucky, and of the gratification they get from both work and family. Theirs is not a lowered or absent commitment but a different kind of commitment that challenges, at least implicitly, the conventional politics of time that continues to shape work and family commitments for most employees.

To label female part-time technical professionals as "traditional," as having withdrawn from work, wanting jobs rather than careers, is to ignore their own perception that they consciously choose to remain at work because it is central to their sense of self. Whereas "traditional" women value family over work, part-time technical professionals value both work and family. They value their ability to enjoy the benefits of both, and have deliberately *chosen* to do both. The identities these women are constructing for themselves are often new assemblages, made up of bits and pieces of the old cloth. It is in part built of a contemporary discourse of self-actualization—note the way child raising and work share a language of satisfaction and job interest—but these are technical professionals in the Midwest and not prone to excessive therapeutic talk. Instead, they struggle to insist that, yes, they have a career—just a different kind of career; and yes, they want to be moms—just not all the time. Moreover, they hold both of these stories to be true, though they sometimes tell them at different times to different people.[5]

5. Thompson and Bunderson (2001) contend that when people spend time in identity-affirming activities, they are less likely to feel conflicting demands on

In reflecting on the relationship between the mothers who make up the largest group in our sample and the other part-timers who have other reasons for reducing work hours, we are struck both by a significant difference between the two groups and by the similarity that lies behind the difference. The mothers, in choosing to be part-time technical professionals, are doing battle with two greedy institutions, each of which presents itself as the primary determinant of who one is. Professional work clearly makes this claim to one's time and self; but so does motherhood. The fact that working mothers must wrestle with both sets of demands to get what they really want (which is a redefined version of both) tends to make them more aware of the possibility of having a life that is not dominated by a single identity.

At the same time, by focusing on the satisfying aspects of bringing up children, the mothers use a language about their nonwork time that links them to the nonmothers we talked with. All of the people we met talk about their work as something gratifying that they want to retain without letting it take over their lives completely. And all of them talked about their various nonwork activities—traveling, dancing, prairie-burning, recording music, volunteering, acting . . . raising children—as worthwhile and life-enhancing activities. What they are struggling to create is new identities in a world that does not yet provide the institutional framework to give those identities easily recognizable names.[6] They are also trying to escape from the tyranny of single identities. Just as Judith Butler (1990) argues that she has to be able to perform each of her multiple identities—academic, woman, lesbian—in its appropriate context, so our respondents claim the right to play their professional role at work, their mom role with their children, their activist role with their peers, and their retiree role with their families and friends, without any identity in any way challenging their right to perform their other identities in different contexts.

---

their time. But their analysis emphasizes that one identity tends to be dominant. We found that many part-timers are rejecting precisely this one-dimensional kind of identity: the time conflicts they experienced as full-timers were the result of their efforts to be more than one thing simultaneously, neither of which was of less importance to them than the other.

6. For a more elaborate discussion of the construction of identity, see Ricoeur 1992, Beck 1992, Somers 1994, and Giddens 1991.

Perhaps it is time to recognize that one can think of oneself as a professional without conjuring up the image of the country doctor delivering babies on Christmas Eve; or that one can have a career without committing oneself to be on the job 24/7 or to wanting to climb a career ladder to the corner office. Time, also, to suggest that taking care of children can be a satisfying activity that does not have to be combined with full-time domesticity and a life of service to the family. As we shall see, it is not always easy to put together the resources to nurture this new vision. Too many workplaces and too many families find the old ways easier. Demanding that commitment to the organization be made visible by a display of conspicuous time-giving is a time-honored practice and relatively simple to implement. The alternatives, as we shall see, are sometimes more complex.

These issues do not always have simple solutions, but at least in their own eyes the people we talked with have begun the process. Rejecting the false dichotomies of professional and dilettante, dedicated careerist and housewife, they argue that one can not only *do* both but also *be* both.

4

"Can You Do That?"

Part-Time Work in

Organizations

Whenever we talk with technical professionals about our research, especially when the audience consists largely of women, they are immediately interested but skeptical: "Do you mean there are engineers working part-time in real jobs?"; "There aren't any programmers working part-time here, but let me know when you find some, I'll apply"; "I just wish"; "I'd love that opportunity"; "Can you do that?" Even within companies where we interviewed successful part-timers, firms with progressive reputations and supposedly well-publicized programs for flexible work, the surprise and skepticism remained. "Is it for real?" "Does it *really* work?" Customized work time is clearly an attractive option, but it is equally clear that arranging it is not always easy, even in companies with nationally recognized work-family policies.

Many of the people we talked with become independent contractors to pursue the kind of balanced professional work they loved. Those who seek work as corporate part-timers sometimes have a more difficult task. They often have to pioneer the new arrangements; if not as solo explorers, then at least as part of a small band of adventurers seeking to colonize a new terrain. Just as they struggle to reconstruct a new kind of professional identity, so they struggle to create the arrangements that allow them to practice it.

"How I Made It Work for Me"

For Alison, a computer specialist, reducing her work time proved comparatively easy. Once she made her decision to go back to work part-time, she simply told her manager about her plans and he made the appropriate arrangements. She is fortunate. She not only works for a large company that prides itself on its progressive work-family policies, she also has a supportive manager:

> It wasn't really a problem. We'd discussed it before I took maternity leave, and he said to just tell him as soon as I'd made the decision. He's known as being very supportive of his part-time programmers, not like some of the other managers, and there were already two others doing it in the department. It helps that he's always looking for good programmers.

She works in the programming unit of a large retail firm that does not have the glamour of some of the high-tech companies, so keeping good programmers is always a high priority. She also benefits from the strong demand for technical professionals of all kinds, and for women in particular. Because they have to overcome a variety of formidable obstacles, women in technical professions tend to be highly qualified (McIlwee and Robinson 1992). Companies are often especially keen to keep them, especially since, as several women note, they have invested substantial time and resources in recruiting and developing them. As Tina, a female engineer, remarks, "They've got a big investment in me and I'm good. They don't want to lose me." The need to retain good employees in a tight labor market has always proved a strong incentive for employers to make arrangements they would otherwise consider unthinkable.

Moreover, corporations are under pressure to diversify their technical staffs. Some of the pressure is internally generated, some of it imposed by government policy. Particularly for those with government contracts (such as those in defense, a sector that employs significant numbers of technical professionals in the United States), the pressure to recruit and retain women is considerable. Nancy, another engineer, acknowledges that

> EO [equal opportunity] does come into it somewhat. Keeping you on the books, for instance. I applied for a contractor position because I

didn't need benefits, and they strongly encouraged me, through giving me a very nice pay raise, to take a part-time position. Because from a government perspective, even though I'm not acting as a senior manager, that's what my grade level is on the books. And it was, frankly, part of our consideration—I have a little bit more job security than my husband does because I'm a woman.

In this field, women at this level are scarce and companies need to retain women employees if for no other reason than to make their numbers look good.

Having something that companies need ensures that these women are in a strong bargaining position when it comes to negotiating part-time work. It also gives them a sense of security that the company is willing to help them make the arrangement work and take them back full-time should they so wish. Lynn, an engineer, notes how her expertise overcame her employer's reluctance: "And I went home and thought about it, and said, 'I'm going to have to quit, it's just not working.' And they agreed to part-time, extremely reluctantly and angrily, and 'We're going to have to hire someone to do your work and this isn't what we want but you're a good employee. We don't want to lose you.' And grumble, grumble." She said later that she is unique because she is the company's expert on heat transference. Because all the work in the area comes to her, she is just too valuable to lose.

Not everyone has it so easy. Natalie, another engineer, found it much more difficult, even though she works for the same company. "It wasn't easy talking them into it. I had to go to HR to get the policy and show it to him. Even when I told him I would quit and complain, he kept putting off telling me it was OK. Eventually a friend told me about a position in another part of the company where the manager was more friendly to part-time work and I just transferred." Natalie is not alone in having difficulty. Even in companies with formal policies, individual managers vary dramatically in their attitudes toward part-time work. Even when the human resources manager is very sympathetic, individual managers may be much less so, with the result that employees who want part-time work have to shop around for an agreeable manager.

For Alice, an engineer who worked in a research laboratory, this variation in managerial responses came as a pleasant surprise:

I did my master's in engineering management through the on-site program into management. Then I had my first child. I took six months'
leave of absence. I thought my career was over. I would come back
after six months and they would put me in a corner somewhere to do
my work. While I was away, a new manager came in; I talked to him
and he told me there was no way a part-timer could be in management. So that reinforced my feeling. Then I was approached by another division. They offered me a role as a project manager part-time.

Alice has benefited from the shortage of good high-tech workers,
which encourages progressive managers to look for good people who
may be dissatisfied elsewhere in the company. One manager told us
informally that his reputation around the company as being favorable to part-timers helps him get good people from other divisions.

For others we interviewed, the issue is a matter not simply of being
able to work part-time but of obtaining work of appropriate quality.
June, a computer professional, had no problem securing a part-time position when she came back from maternity leave, but it was harder to
find one where she would be given interesting and responsible work.

I really wasn't doing the same kind of work, I was not supervising
anybody. That first year I was basically given menial tasks. It was
rather frustrating. I finally complained. In the meantime, we got a
new manager. So I went to him, it was a man this time, and told him
my frustrations. That I felt I could definitely handle more responsibilities, and he was rather floored that I was doing what I had been doing
for the past year. So he looked for another assignment for me outside
the department. . . . It sounded interesting and I almost took it, but at
the same time a new opportunity was coming up under this manager
and he offered me an assignment doing that.

As she indicates, having a woman manager does not necessarily indicate a more favorable response to requests for part-time work.
What matters is the attitude of the particular manager.

Sometimes the emergent informal network of part-time professionals in the company helps prepare a newcomer to part-time work
like Tina for what to expect:

First, I talked to another woman I knew who was working part-time.
What she suggested to me was that I come up with a job that I could

do part-time. Then, rather than just go to my boss and say, "I want to work part-time," I could say, "You have this job that needs to get done and I could do it working part-time." So I did. And it was OK with him. He agreed to that for an indefinite period of time and I worked twenty hours a week.

In the absence of well-established, thoroughly institutionalized practices, taking the initiative is often an important part of the process. One of the reasons many people were so willing to talk to us was that they wanted to share their experiences, to show others how it is done.

Managers' reluctance to go along with requests for part-time schedules is not just a matter of personal prejudice. Sometimes even companies with permissive formal policies have other policies that, whether by design or not, place obstacles in the way. Policies that shape managers' own self-interest, for example, can have a direct effect on how they treat their employees. Some companies allocate managers a specific number of employees or "heads" for their unit and count a part-time employee as one head. Susan, an engineer for an automobile company, describes the contradictory situation at her workplace:

You can arrange it so that if there's somebody else that wants to come part-time and it's a job that really doesn't have five days of work, we can get hold of somebody and arrange something and it's up to the management to hire both of you to share the job. The only downfall is, as a part-time person, you're still counted as a full head, so some people with head-count restraints would rather have a full-time person than a part-time person. You're still counted as a full head.

Given the intense pressure to lower head counts as a way of cutting costs, managers are willing to allow a part-time schedule only when they desperately want to keep a particular employee. It is certainly not an arrangement they agree to routinely.

Sometimes an employer's reluctance to accommodate part-time employees translates into a suggestion that the employee become an independent contractor. Several employers routinely require that individuals who want to go from full-time to part-time status be reclassified as "peripheral" or "temporary" support (often with a corresponding loss of status and benefits). This is particularly the case for older technical professionals who continue to work for their employer on a part-time basis, but are allowed to do so only as contractors.

This norm of full-time work is particularly constraining when one seeks a new job. Only one of our respondents had been hired to work part-time without having first proved her worth to the company, and she was an experienced professional with an active port-folio of visible achievement. Demonstrated reliability and perform-ance seem to be a sine qua non of part-time employment in professional-level jobs. A female engineer told us, "I've had man-agers tell me that I've been able to do what I've been doing because of the reputation I've built up over fifteen years. There's no ques-tion, I could not come in from scratch and do this." From the em-ployer's point of view, she had established that she was a good, loyal employee and could thus be trusted to work in unconventional ways. Past corporate performance serves as an easily read profes-sional portfolio.

Karen, a part-time computer professional who has been able to design her own job, thinks an inexperienced worker might not be able to cope with the degree of autonomy she enjoys:

> I'd worked for a long time before I came into the situation, having as free a hand as I do. I now report to the VP for university libraries. Ours is much more of a collaborative effort than a supervisor/supervisee re-lationship, and I'd say that's also true for the VP for information ser-vices, it's always been more collaborative than supervisor/supervisee. But, you know, part of this is my age. I mean I was forty-five when I started working for the university. And I'd had a number of years of experience before I did that, so I'm much more capable in many ways of taking on a position like this, or creating a position like this. One of the big things I was told when I was in management school, they re-ally should require any kid who comes into management school to have two years of experience first. Because I could run circles around them in terms of having my logic set up, my problem-solving skills in place, and knowing where the hell I wanted to go with it. And the same is true in this kind of job. I had enough experience before I came into this situation so I was able to cope with being basically put out there and told "Do your thing," without anybody having any idea what my thing was supposed to be.

For Karen, the issue is professional expertise and experience, but for many others it is clearly demonstrated loyalty to the organization.

Because of the difficulty of getting an unconventional job, gratitude is a theme that runs through many interviews. Nancy, who traded her managerial position for a part-time computer engineering job, notes how good her company was during her pregnancy:

> I, unfortunately, was one of the women who were extremely sick during pregnancy. I could throw up thirty times a day for nine months. I didn't believe in stopping after the first trimester. That turned into a real problem after two or three months, and everybody was saying, "Are you sure you shouldn't go to the hospital?" because I was so sick. Then I decided that we should tell them. We had wanted to wait. I would say that my immediate boss was extremely displeased at the fact that I was pregnant, because of the fact that this was a new business unit I was heading up, and they were going to have to find someone to replace me. Near the end of the pregnancy, I was put on bed rest and the company was fantastic. I would come in as much as I could, and the rest I stayed home, and they paid my salary even when they knew I was not returning. They ended up determining that the reason I was so sick was that my gall bladder had failed. They scheduled me for surgery and I was not returning after the surgery, and they still went ahead and gave me full benefits throughout the surgery as well as sick leave after it, when technically they were well aware I was not coming back. That would not have been the norm. Those types of things created in me a real sense of loyalty to the company.

Barbara, another engineer, expresses a similar sense of gratitude, despite a degree of cynicism about how enlightened her employer actually is:

> While you're part-time, though, you're not going to even consider going anyplace else. Nobody else is going to hire you part-time, so it's a real benefit, and I'm real grateful. . . . The sense is, and I don't know how much of this is based on actual fact, the perception is that they won't hire you at part-time. The part-time is a benefit for being a good employee, it's just to help them out temporarily in a situation, not as a career option.

Our part-time workers' gratitude to their employers, coupled with their innate professionalism, ensures that most of them work extremely hard to prove their worth. As Lynn put it, "I have the feeling that working part-time, you actually get more done with your time because you are so limited in these three days . . . you're very efficient." Amelia, a technical writer, agrees: "They just can't understand that someone might be able to get it done in thirty-five hours, or twenty-four, or thirty-two, for that matter. So unfortunately, I had to prove to them that I could get things done in less time." This concern to be productive stems in part from a continued perception of a "normal" work load as consuming 40 to 50 hours a week. This is the "work" that has to be done. Although they have managed to negotiate a reduced load, many still find it difficult to see "full-time" as a socially produced work load, as arbitrary as any other.

Once arrangements are made, however, there are few complaints. As we have seen, these people like their work. They are strongly attracted to technical work per se; they enjoy working on technical projects, solving technical problems. In sharp contrast to professionals such as attorneys (Epstein et al. 1999), most part-time technical professionals continue to have interesting, varied, and challenging jobs. While some of our respondents told us that their choice to reduce their work hours has altered the kind of work they do, they are virtually unanimous in claiming that their assignments are not less challenging. Even when they are not doing precisely the same work they did as full-timers, technical work remains creative work, requiring knowledge and autonomy. Employers cannot easily routinize the work and assign the least attractive portions to part-timers. Zoë, a computer scientist for a major retailer, says: "I was given a few simple jobs when I first started part-time but now I am doing the same work as everyone else. It's interesting stuff." Angela has even more positive things to say: "The work's pretty interesting around here. We do the programming for all the new systems. I wouldn't be here if the work wasn't challenging. This stuff is really fun only when you're doing new stuff. My boss knows I'm good so he won't waste me on the routine stuff." Part-time work can be interesting work.

Our respondents' search for satisfying professional work has been successful. They are able to keep the kind of technically interesting work for which they trained. Of course, they are a self-selected sample. Given the importance of interesting work to their identities, those who could obtain only routine work as part-timers would probably have stayed home altogether or gone back to work full-time to pursue more interesting work. Nonetheless, we did expect to hear some complaints about the quality of the work, since that complaint was almost routine among the part-time lawyers with whom Cynthia Epstein and her colleagues spoke. We did not. All the technical professionals we talked with have been able to find work that satisfies their needs.

We originally expected that official company policy would determine opportunities for part-time work, and it is true that in individual negotiation a company's policy is important. When it comes to the final decision, however, the critical factors are the perceptions of individual managers and individual employees. In fact, employers often go out of their way to insist on the exceptional nature of each individual arrangement to ensure it does not set too firm a precedent. This finding, that individual managers rather than formal company policies are critical in facilitating part-time work, is not new. It is sometimes dismissed, however, as a by-product of a faulty implementation scheme or poor education on the part of the human resources department, with the corollary that a new generation of more progressive managers will solve the problem.

This assumption is overoptimistic. Nearly all official company policies, however progressive, leave ultimate discretion to the individual manager, and deliberately so. It is part of a more general policy that requires each request for customized work arrangements to be treated as an exceptional case. The only circumstance that comes close to wide acceptance as a legitimate reason to request part-time status is the obligations of parenthood, and only for a woman. Several respondents suggested that this attitude reflects both the cultural acceptance of women's "sacrifice" of career to family and employers' desire to retain scarce female employees in whom they have invested considerable resources. It seems to us, however, that it also reflects the view that women are not normal employees, and that treating them differently does not upset the normal ways of doing business. For men, only making a transition to retirement

comes close to being a generally accepted rationale for seeking reduced time, but here again, each case is treated individually.[1]

"It's Not Possible in All Jobs"

Although the corporate employees we talked with are very happy
with their own jobs, most of them are unwilling to generalize their
experiences. They often put their success in getting good part-time
work down to good luck, a cooperative manager, or their own special talents. They all have tales to tell of friends in other companies,
or even in other departments of their own firms, who have not been
able to secure part-time work. But perhaps more important, they
often see real constraints, often technical ones, that would prevent
part-time arrangements from working in other settings. Since these
hard constraints figure prominently in many justifications for limiting customized work, it is worth exploring them in some detail.

Most of these constraints center on the difficulties of working
part-time in settings where others are working longer and more inflexible hours. Tight deadlines and inflexible work rhythms, for example, are often mentioned as making particular jobs difficult to
customize. Since many of our respondents work a shortened workweek, they may be away from their work for three, four, or even five
consecutive days. If such lengthy interruptions require time to be
wasted reviewing past work or redoing some portion of the job, then
part-time work is difficult. Similarly, if the employee's activities are
tightly coupled to other parts of the organization, concerns that the
intermittent activity of part-time workers may slow the completion
of tasks can discourage employers from authorizing reduced employment. Susan, an engineer for an automobile manufacturer,
points to these types of concerns in explaining why a particular de-

1. We were offered a number of anecdotes about men who reduced their time at
work while they pursued further education but were not seen as working part-time,
though they were paid as such. Because pursuing education is a common career
move in a high-tech firm, it is not seen as a departure from the normal way of doing
business. There are obvious parallels here with the accepted practice of automatically reemploying veterans at their old job level after absence for military service,
or even granting them extra seniority credit, while treating women's absence to
rear their children as a setback to their careers.

partment at her place of employment is more conducive than others to part-time work:

> It's production related but not as closely related as design jobs. There are production deadlines, but not as many of them as in the department designing new parts. They have continuous deadlines they develop on a schedule. Also, there's much more program management involvement with the components, there's a lot more meetings, more regular meetings that you have to go to. With materials, there's not as much.

Many kinds of technical work involve tight deadlines. As deadlines approach, the pace and intensity of work go up and the sense of urgency increases. Part-timers are thus faced with a dilemma: either they must work full-time (or more) for a while to meet the approaching deadline or they must ignore the urgency of the situation and thereby jeopardize the timely completion of the job and risk the resentment of co-workers and management.

Roberta, an engineer for an electronics company, describes the problems when she is faced with deadlines:

> There's a situation that just happened. We did a schedule, our whole team, and we tried to project when I could get certain things done. And it's already slipped two weeks; the problem is when I'm doing something and I don't get the contacts or the cooperation from other people and I just have two days in the office to work on it, you know, if that doesn't get done on the two days I'm here, then it slips like a whole other week rather than another two days.

In this case, a job-share might well resolve the issue; but June, a computer professional working for a large retailer, finds that sharing a job creates other difficulties:

> And so she [her manager] was getting ready to take her leave when I suggested that I and another part-timer—she was working five half-days—I suggested that we share the job as a temporary solution while our manager was gone, since they weren't going to replace her for just three months. She was only going to take a three-month leave. I said why not have her and me job-share? And be managers over, at that time there were about six people. Lo and behold, it was approved. I was

surprised. It was tough, managing a team. I think I learned a lot from it. The other girl finally went three days a week to make it easier. The problem was the Wednesday, the day we shared, we spent the entire day in meetings. Our systems manager would schedule the weekly status meeting that day because we were both there. Then after lunch we would hold a staff meeting of our people. And then we'd have maybe half an hour to discuss what she had done Monday and Tuesday. Thursday and Friday, I felt that all I did was clean up the stuff she had started. I'd leave notes for her on Monday, I'd come in on Wednesday and she hadn't done anything. It might have been her, I don't know, but she was very much her own person. She wanted to be totally in charge. With me as her backup, I guess. I kept trying to get out of it. And I was told if I wasn't managing anymore, then they couldn't justify my part-time position. So it was either take this or leave it.

Such problems with job-sharing have been well documented (Meier 1978, Nollen 1982); it is not a panacea. Ironically, however, this case also presents evidence that organizations sometimes force part-timers into managerial positions despite the widespread view that the two cannot mix.

Our respondents identify a variety of other time-related factors that create problems for part-time workers, especially those with children. One is the need for travel. While travel is not an insuperable difficulty, it may well conflict with nonwork activities since there is no guarantee that the timing of trips will be convenient. Several of our respondents report refusing jobs that involve significant amounts of travel for this reason. Others, like Barbara, the computer engineer, accept it but find it inconvenient in various ways: "I do a lot of traveling, but if there's somebody else around who can do it, I would just as soon step aside and let somebody else do it. And it never fails that my husband and I are asked to travel on the same day. And we call upon one of the grandmothers to take care of the kids." The need for travel is part of a more general problem, the need to work unusual or unpredictable hours, since part-timers, like full-time employees, often have to coordinate their child care arrangements with others.

Of course, if one can choose the hours one works, odd hours need not be a problem. Many of our respondents, especially those who combine homework with child care, report that they work what most people would consider unusual schedules: from four until eight in the morning, say, then another hour in the evening. When the job dictates an inflexible schedule of work hours, however, problems easily develop, even when the required hours are conventional. Even some contractors feel compelled to be "at work" during conventional work hours because clients expect to be able to call them during office hours.

Some jobs require irregular schedules that can be extremely difficult to synchronize with the kinds of activities that motivate reduced work arrangements in the first place. Ellen, an engineer, points to laboratory work as a prime example: "Any time you write the code, you have to go into the lab and test. And the way the hierarchy with lab time is, the developer is always last in line, so you'll end up with night lab hours, midnight, and weekend lab hours, and the Friday after Thanksgiving. And things like that." For many of those we talked with, these "normal" rhythms of work put obstacles in the way of more customized work arrangements.

An important part of the normal rhythm of work is the need to cooperate and coordinate with other employees. Some jobs (and some workplaces) involve large numbers of meetings. Mandatory meetings create problems, either because part-timers have to rearrange their schedules to avoid missing them or because a team includes more than one part-timer and it is virtually impossible to find a meeting time at which all team members can be present. Pressures to be physically present—or at least to be on call—increase when a part-timer possesses unique expertise, especially when deadlines reduce the slack in the system. This is the problem that faces Ron, a computer professional:

> Some of the technical jobs, you need to be there. Like LAN administration, you need to wear a pager, because if something needs to be fixed, you need to be there to fix it, you can't say I'll get it tomorrow. Some jobs definitely do not work part-time, unless you're willing to be on call during those off hours. Then it would work, but usually you have to be on site.

Note his assumption that the work will be left undone if the part-timer is not there to do it.

A related problem arises with managerial positions. Several corporate part-timers point to an unwritten rule that part-timers cannot be promoted into management. We met several people who were obliged to "trade down" out of a managerial position to get their employers to agree to let them work part-time. Yet what is the principal obstacle to reduced work in management? Only one respondent sees it as inherent in the actual work of managers, the necessity to supervise some employees constantly. Virtually everyone else points to the necessity of attending meetings. Particularly in matrix organizations, but also in more conventional ones, managers are expected to be on site at all times and to attend frequent meetings.

Most of the people we talked with felt that working part-time limits opportunities for promotion into management. In some cases, promotion to high rank is perceived as restricted to those who give all their time to the corporation. More often, however, the limitation is part of a set of beliefs about what *kinds* of work can be done by part-timers and what cannot. Management for most technical professionals is not just a promotion in the way that, say, making partner is for a lawyer. It marks a transition to a different kind of work, albeit one that traditionally marks a promotion up the corporate career ladder (Whalley 1986).

Finally, Roberta, the engineer, notes that starting a new job on a part-time basis can make the need for cooperation particularly intense and problematic:

> One of the things my boss and I talked about is that when I'm in, we have a team meeting and I'm involved in that. But she and I don't have a lot of one on one, because I'm not here that often and she's busy. She's promised to do more one-on-one time with me. Because I am learning a new job, going from being a systems engineer to more of a marketing role, and I don't have an MBA. She has an MBA and she's like five levels above me, so I could be learning more from her.

Time constraints can be particularly onerous in such situations, where desirable but not absolutely necessary tasks tend to get postponed indefinitely.

The electronic-communication revolution is supposed to facilitate just this kind of informal contact. E-mail, cell phones, faxes, and the like are supposed to make much of this interaction available beyond the constraints of time and space. Nonetheless, even professionals working on their own, connected by sophisticated electronic equipment, find they cannot be totally isolated. They feel they need to do a certain amount of "face work" to assert their commitment to the workplace and to reduce the resentment of colleagues and supervisors. Perhaps unsurprisingly for technical professionals, however, many of our respondents are likely to see this requirement as political rather than technical.

Some of our respondents do perceive physical presence as a real requirement. Tina notes that the two partners in a job-sharing arrangement need to meet face to face: "That's when we can talk and make sure we are on the same wavelength and make any decisions that we think need to be joint." When technical professionals report that they need to go to at least some meetings and find it hard to work entirely in isolation, they confirm what students of electronic communication and remote work have been arguing for some time. Homework, even when mediated electronically, appears to be limited by the fact that visibility and interaction with co-workers are important parts of building a viable career (Olson 1989). Electronic communication, even when highly sophisticated, appears to be far less suited to creative, agenda-setting work than face-to-face meetings and brainstorming (McKenney, Zack, and Doherty 1992; Nohria and Eccles 1992).

This belief that most of the limits on the spread of part-time work result from hard technical and organizational requirements minimizes any criticism that might otherwise be directed at companies and individual managers for not making such work more widely available. As other studies suggest (Mackenzie 1990, Whalley 1986b), technical people often make a sharp distinction between technical requirements that they consider real and necessary and managerial decisions that they consider political and malleable. As long as the 50-hour workweek is taken as a technical requirement rather than a political one, working any less will continue to be seen as an unusual option, available only in unusual circumstances.

Overcoming Barriers

Even though our respondents emphasize the importance of hard technical and organizational constraints and are often grateful for their own good luck, many of their experiences suggest that these perceptions are too pessimistic. Some are already pioneering strategies that have rolled back those "hard" limits. The experiences of others indicate the possibility of other reforms that might expand significantly the range of jobs amenable to customized work arrangements. There may be hard, practical limits to the spread of such arrangements, but these limits may not lie precisely where they appear to be in existing organizations.[2]

If, for example, organizational cycles of high and low demand for time correspond with the cyclical pattern of other spheres of life, they may actually be desirable rather than inimical to part-time work, as Danielle, an engineer employed by a telecommunications company, points out:

> One of the things I think made it work is the kind of job I did was cyclical, in that there were things that you did, some applications would need to be written, you needed to work really hard for a month or something like that, and then there would be a period that would kind of taper off a little bit and you know, I would be able to have more time to enjoy my children. By chance, it seemed to work out that the heavy loads were in the winter and the light loads were in the summer, which is nice. I had time with my kids then.

The timing of surges of work that Danielle attributes to chance may even be subject to human control. Margaret, another engineer with a large electronics company, says that she and her co-workers can anticipate the need for bursts of effort months in advance because their managers "get these little powwows together" where they talk about upcoming deadlines and exhort employees to "push." Discretionary behavior on the part of managers, customers, or others could help part-timers manage the problem of deadlines and work cycles.

Similarly, not everyone sees the need for cooperation and coordination as a major problem. Indeed, at least one engineer, Ellen, ar-

---

2. The fact that what appear to be unalterable barriers to part-time work may be socially constructed is also supported by Leslie Perlow (2001), whose cross-cultural comparisons of the organization of software engineering indicate that there are, in fact, different ways of organizing technical work and that these different modes of organization have different implications for flexible employment practices.

gues that the team character of work can be an advantage: "That worked out really well, everything was based on a team; there were very few things you were individually responsible for. You'd break things up and you would have individual sections that you were assigned. And that way I could always take more or less, depending on how much time they had and how well I knew the areas." Ellen also notes that teamwork creates opportunities for co-workers to cover for one another. If employers are willing to assign work that requires expertise in a certain area to two or more persons, one person is never solely responsible.

Even the oft-cited meeting problem can be attended to with the appropriate imagination and cooperation. Several of our respondents find that it is perfectly possible to manage without attending meetings or to attend meetings without being a full-time employee. Nancy, an engineer who works part-time and largely at home, finds herself being drawn back into project management by her employer, a software company (and a matrix organization). Meetings are scheduled for the days she comes in and she makes herself available by phone in case a conference call is needed. While she doesn't feel she is the best choice for a managerial role, she finds that she can deal with the meetings:

> Before, without the project management, I would go in once a month, because my husband can take in my time card. I didn't have as much need to be there. But now doing project management, I have stepped up to four times a month, which initially I was not as comfortable with, but my son is older now and much happier, actually, going to play at somebody's house. So it was me having that trouble letting go versus him [laugh]. So yes, I go in once a week right now, and let people know that's when I'm there, and given enough foreknowledge, they can tend to schedule around that.
>
> I'll tell you there are probably ten meetings that I'm invited to and I choose not to go to the majority of them. Now I do have another person on the team who is the backup. If there is a critical meeting and I can't make it because I'm not working that day or whatever, he goes. So we can kind of tag-team it. When I took the position, I said to my boss, "I don't think this is a match for a part-time person. You need to have a backup person identified, and you need to go to the other project managers and the business unit leader and say, 'Nancy is only going to be available at these times. We still think she's the best choice, please be aware of how this is going to limit our ability to interact.'"

This extensive account suggests that many meetings can be avoided and delegation is possible. It also shows that if an employer really wants a part-timer to manage, a combination of organizational effort and individual adjustment, neither of which involves radical changes in the way things work, can make part-time management feasible.

Electronic communications can facilitate these adjustments. Though they do not completely substitute for face-to-face interaction, many of our respondents do make extensive use of such media to reduce work and increase flexibility. Electronic mail, for example, is widely used as a means of staying accessible and of doing work at odd hours at home. Others maintain regular telephone contact with co-workers, even when they are not formally at work. By accepting and even inviting calls at home, part-timers can reduce cooperation and deadline problems. They can also create more opportunities to work off site; one woman describes participating in a three-hour conference call with Japanese customers while playing catch with her daughter. Amelia, another technical writer employed by an electronics company that had space problems, found her employer was willing to provide her with a home computer and a tape drive so that she could do documentation work at her house.

Sometimes this integration is seamless. As Irene, who logs in on her (unpaid) days at home, puts it:

> They didn't know I was part-time because I was so responsible at times. And so they asked me to review their design on a day that I'm not in. They asked my supervisor, for some reason, not me. And she responded back, with a copy to me, "She's not in those days, try to reschedule on another day." And that was a real good sign for me. I said, "I never told you guys, I work part-time." They were like "We never knew, we got answers from you all the time."

Here the technology all but requires the employee to do unpaid work in order to maintain her professional commitment to her job. Andrea says:

> They can phone questions to me, or they can e-mail me. At work everyone usually has their office number listed, I have my home

phone number listed. It's the personal home number, so even Mondays when I'm not working I take phone calls like that. And there's e-mail. Even on days I don't work sometimes I log in just to read my e-mail to see if there's anything important. Sometimes if you wait from Friday till the following Wednesday to work again, the e-mail can really build up, so I'll log in on other days just for that.

This strategy comes close to making electronic communication an "electronic leash," as one of our respondents put it, compelling more work even when the employee is not being paid to work. Nonetheless, as a component of customized work arrangements that facilitate more off-site work and provide some of the necessary coordination, electronic communications do offer the possibility of extending customized work arrangements.

While some part-timers use electronic tools to reduce the need to be on site, others seek to persuade their managers that their presence is not as necessary as they think. Many of our respondents are quite skeptical of the need to be physically present in the office. The job-sharers Jennifer and Lisa point out that they hardly see their managers even though they work on site: "I think about the fact that my manager is in another building and I maybe see him— because of the way the organization is—I maybe see him once a month." Amelia talks about the various kinds of face work she is able to do, so that she appears to be on site more than she actually is: "I do try to make a team meeting every other week. I do make a special effort to talk to my boss or leave her a voice mail at least once a day, so that she doesn't forget, or doesn't feel like I'm not letting her know what I'm doing." Still others note that managers' concern about productivity at home is misplaced, as they find that they actually get more done away from the distractions of the office, a view that finds ample support in the literature (Williams 2000).

Face time and networking may sometimes be important in getting professional work done, even if they are not always acknowledged as work by those who engage in them. Epstein and her colleagues (1999) argue that part-time lawyers regret missing out on opportunities for socialization and are hindered by their inability to participate equally in networking. For contractors, as we shall see, this is a real problem, but salaried technical professionals do not experience the pressure to generate business that makes networking

essential. Nor are they focused on achieving upward career mobility, an emphasis that would have made socializing with superiors,
networking, and politicking crucial. In the absence of these pressures, salaried technical professionals in particular are quite likely
to dismiss face time and networking as irritating and ultimately unnecessary parts of getting their job done.

Employers sometimes share in these demonstrations that "hard
limits" are in fact negotiable. Both June, the computer professional,
and Nancy, the engineer, had been pressured to take on managerial
duties after having been told that such arrangements were not possible. In effect, they discovered that negotiations over part-time
arrangements can be a two-way street. Employees are forced to bar-
gain for individual variations to standard work arrangements; but
when managers need or want something, they, too, may wind up
bargaining, demonstrating thereby that organizational time can be
made flexible when there is the will to do so.

Without stretching the argument too far and insisting that all
"hard" constraints are simply unnecessary roadblocks to be wished
away with the right attitude and goodwill, we must note that many
constraints seem harder in some situations than in others. For every
person who sees the need to attend meetings as an impediment to
part-time work there is another who has found that prior coordination or the use of new technology makes such arrangements perfectly functional. Technical constraints on the expansion of customized work arrangements are not as hard as they often seem.
Difficulties in arranging part-time work are as much a function of
managers' reluctance to normalize part-time work as of technical
necessity.

Why So Difficult?

If people can work part-time in many more circumstances than
most people—including some of our respondents—believe, why
hasn't part-time work become more available? Why does each negotiation seemingly have to proceed as though it were unique? Such
systematic difficulties generally indicate that something more is
going on than simple conservatism on the part of managers. One answer lies in the one kind of constraint that seems almost impossible

to overcome: the need for managers to know and trust employees before they allow part-time work. The reasons for the reluctance to expand part-time opportunities, we suggest, lie in issues of control.

Working long hours in an all-embracing corporate culture that opens up the possibility of a long-term climb up the organizational ladder is the traditional package that technical professionals—especially engineers—have been sold to ensure their loyalty. To manage technical staff performing expert, discretionary work that is difficult or impossible to supervise directly, companies have offered a "loyalty package" to ensure they get the best work from their technical staff. Some versions stress the long hours—the new company town—with the toys and technical thrills to maintain motivation. Others—IBM was always the traditional exemplar—stress the long-term career rewards for loyalty to the organization.

Part-time work threatens these traditional structures of regulation and control. When it is portrayed as more suitable for practitioners than for managers, as it usually is, opportunities for promotion can no longer serve to motivate and discipline technical staff. A similar problem is created if face time or other forms of organizational time are cut back. Time, as Eviator Zerubavel (1987) points out, is an important currency that we bestow on those we think deserve it. When employees signal that they wish to curtail their gift of time to the organization, it may be interpreted as a signal that the organization deserves less from them than their other commitments. When management demands time, it is often demanding a display of commitment and loyalty rather than simply insisting on time worked for money paid. Cynthia Epstein and her colleagues (1999) observed young corporate lawyers going out of their way to be seen working late, even spending normal work hours in the gym or doing personal work in order to do so. Long hours are seen as a proxy for commitment to the organization. Part-timers, of necessity, are going to fall short in this respect.

Paradoxically, the opportunity for part-time work can itself serve as a motivational tool, but only if it is hard to get. The gratitude and hard work that part-timers display are a function of part-time work's rarity. If it becomes routine, it will no longer be available as part of the repertoire of managerial rewards. In one stroke, normalizing part-time work would remove two powerful company mechanisms of control: the use of extended hours as an indicator of a professional's commitment to the organization and the use of reduced hours as a reward and a benefit.[3]

Part-Time Work as a Privilege

A striking feature of our respondents' accounts is the highly individualized nature of their arrangements. When they first sought to negotiate part-time work, many felt that they were reinventing the wheel, unaware that others in the company had also sought or arranged part-time work. Indeed, we were often asked about our own knowledge of employees in similar circumstances. Though they enjoy their own jobs and often make use of innovative mechanisms to make them work, many feel that technical constraints on extending part-time work are hard, and thus their own experiences cannot be generalized. All the same, they are eager to share their experiences. One reason people often gave for talking with us was a desire to share their often hard-won information so that others could benefit and gain the advantages that they enjoyed so much themselves.

Employers, on the contrary, seem to have little interest in normalizing customized work-time arrangements. Their interest is in maintaining control over when and to whom they give the "privilege" of working part-time. Employers will offer it to individuals with particular kinds of expertise or to particular categories of employees, such as mothers, but they do not want to normalize it, because it would then undermine the standard package of corporate professional rewards. Thus it is particularly difficult for men to secure part-time corporate employment: they remain the model for "normal" work arrangements even as their numerical dominance diminishes.

Organizations continue to be uncomfortable with the idea of abandoning standardized hierarchical arrangements and allowing even experienced employees this degree of latitude, even though technical work has long posed this kind of dilemma for employers. Technical work has always resisted the kind of detailed control and

---

3. We have developed this argument in greater detail in Meiksins and Whalley 2001.

standardization that characterized manual and clerical work for much of the twentieth century. Career hierarchies and salary and benefit packages were designed largely to create conditions under which employers could trust such workers to carry out their responsibilities loyally. The package having served companies well for nearly a century, most are reluctant to lose any part of it.

Its days may be drawing to a close, however. Contemporary organization theorists point out that modern organizations are in flux and must learn to learn and to be flexible (Morgan 1986). An absence of standardization and greater variability may be precisely what is needed, both for organizations and for the people who work in them. The growth of project teams, greater employee turnover, and the flattening of corporate hierarchies all suggest that organizations can no longer rely on the old career structures to ensure company loyalty. Instead, they may be forced to rely on the professional commitment that our part-time workers displayed: a commitment to doing the job right because of their sense of technical and professional responsibility, because—despite their part-time status—being technical professionals is an integral part of their identity.

There is some evidence that companies are moving in this direction. As Nancy DiTomaso (1996) has noted:

> Even corporate workers employed on a permanent, secure basis are increasingly expected to act like subcontracted workers. Employers expect managers and professionals to think of themselves as entrepreneurs or as self-employed, to continually ask how they can add more value to their work organization, and to self monitor, to deeply internalize the viewpoint that they are likely to be retained by the organization only as long as their expertise serves the needs of the organization. (Quoted in Smith 1997)

As we shall see, the growing use of independent contracting in the technical professions reinforces this view.

5

Going It Alone

Most discussions of the effort to control work hours focus on salaried employment. When critics look for explanations of long work hours, they concentrate on the internal dynamics of large organizations: the use of work time as a measure of commitment to the organization, the compulsion to work long hours as a way to move up the organizational ladder. Moreover, solutions to the problems generated by very long work hours are typically framed as "family-friendly policies," policies that organizations undertake to accommodate the need of some of their employees to spend less time at work (at least for a while).

Our interviews reveal the usefulness of looking beyond the organization. Independent professionals, too, are frequently under pressure to work very long hours, and yet some of them have found ways to work less than full-time schedules as contractors and consultants. Moreover, there is frequently a link between part-time contracting and the politics of time in organizations. Some part-time contractors have opted to become independent professionals because it is either the best or the only way for them to achieve control over their time. Even when the decision to become a contractor is not immediately related to issues of time, it often involves a rejection of corporate practices that sometimes turns into a rejection of corporate approaches to time as well.

Until very recently, independent contractors were on the fringe of technical occupations. In engineering in particular they were restricted largely to the lower end of the design sector, and contract programmers were often working for job shops while looking for "real" work. There were a few notable exceptions, a few highly skilled experts brought in at high cost to solve a difficult and rare problem, but that was not the way an engineer typically worked. Engineers have been corporate professionals from the beginning and served as models for the development of the elaborate career structures, long-term contracts, and extensive benefit packages that provided the material base for the modern professional managerial class.

This situation is changing. New organizational structures have emphasized project teams and a lean workforce, both of which encourage the interchangeability of technical staff. Companies still employ core staffs but are far more willing to rely on contractors for flexibility. Self-employment, particularly among women, has been growing, and it is increasingly common for a career to include a stint as an independent contractor. Indeed, in engineering, computer science, and other technical fields, establishing one's own business has even come to be defined as a positive goal, something to which one aspires, an alternative to the modest organizational career (this goal is epitomized in the public eye by the dot-com phenomenon). The emergence of these new organizational structures has also coincided with the emergence of new technical occupations, such as technical writing and computer programming, in which traditional organizational career tracks are not well established. Being an independent is not unusual for practitioners in these fields.

Obviously, most independent contractors do not work part-time. Our sample was deliberately restricted to those who claimed to be reducing their work time. It included technical professionals who chose contracting as a way to achieve a degree of control over their time and others who reduced their work arrangements after they became contractors. They all see their contracting as a source of flexibility rather than instability. To understand the experiences of all part-time technical professionals, not just those who remain in corporate employment, we need to look at the ways in which contractors' experiences resemble and differ from those of salaried employees. The proliferation of opportunities to work as a contractor makes such consideration all the more important.

Going Solo

Independent contracting takes a variety of forms: some contractors work for one company, some for many; some work on site, some off; some take long breaks, others work a shortened workday. None of those we interviewed, however, got their work through agencies, which they often disparagingly called "body shops." Certainly many technical professionals do work through such agencies, which serve as a source of temporary technical help for companies that need additional labor to meet short-term needs, either for extra employees or for specialized expertise. Indeed, this form of work has proliferated in the era of downsizing and corporate reorganization. As with other kinds of labor, organizations find that it is often cheaper to augment their core technical workforce with this kind of short-term agency-mediated staff. To the people we talked with, however, such agencies do not seem to provide an effective mechanism for controlling one's time, since they do not allow contractors to predict when they will be asked to work or for how long. Moreover, many contractors think that if they require unusual schedules, or if they often reject work offered to them, they may be identified as undesirable by the agencies on which they depend. Since our respondents were rarely talking directly from their own experience, they may be exaggerating the problems involved in working though such agencies, particularly for high-tech professionals. These problems are well documented, however, for less skilled temps (Negrey 1993).

Probably the closest thing to "body shop" employment we encountered was the case of two chemical engineers who are working part-time through an agency that supplies employees to a large petrochemical company. Both were originally full-time employees of that petrochemical company. The company in question was not particularly progressive and had no formal policy for allowing part-time work. Moreover, it has undergone a series of workforce reductions in recent years, so that even the more secure full-time employees have become concerned about holding on to their jobs. The company has been making increasing use of contract labor, as it finds that its newly reduced workforce is not always sufficient to get the work done.

Beth, a chemical engineer, had worked for the petrochemical

company for a few years when, in 1986, she decided to cut back to part-time hours after the birth of her second child. She tried working full-time and taking care of two children for several months and found that "I really can't handle this." She approached her boss and asked for a part-time schedule. Although he initially resisted (the company had no part-time engineers, according to Beth, and was reluctant to "set a precedent"), she persisted and eventually was able to get a three-day schedule. After two years as a part-timer, however, she quit. She found that she did not like the work she was doing in the unit to which she had been moved—she wasn't sure if the move had occurred because she was working part-time—and encountered an attractive opportunity to work for a consultant she had met. For several years, this arrangement worked out quite well; she contracted with the consultant and worked about 25 hours a week. In the early 1990s, however, she was pressured to move to employee status and to increase her hours accordingly. In addition, her employer began to experience economic problems and at times she was not paid for her work. Eventually, in 1994, she left. She received a few job offers; but when she called a former colleague for a reference, he suggested working for a contractor who supplied her old employer, the petrochemical company. She decided to do so and wound up as a contractor working approximately 30 hours per week (largely 9 to 3). Beth finds that this kind of "tied contracting" has finally enabled her to obtain a predictable reduced work schedule that also provides stable, rewarding employment.

For the other engineer we met who worked under this kind of arrangement, things are less positive. Sarah has worked for the petrochemical company since 1977. She had wanted to go part-time since 1984, when her first child was born, but her supervisor refused her request. Finally, in 1993, the group for which she was working was disbanded as part of a major shakeup and workforce reduction. Sarah feared she would be laid off or be forced to quit. When she made inquiries, she discovered the possibility of working as a contractor through the agency that had placed Beth. She has been working through the agency for the petrochemical company ever since and has been able to reduce her average weekly workweek to about 20 hours. She complains that her schedule is unpredictable, however, varying tremendously from one week to the next, so that she has little control over when and how much she works. Sarah's experience reveals many of the problems of trying to work part-time through an agency. Beth's case demonstrates that someone who is clearly in demand may still be able to use the agency mechanism to develop a satisfactory reduced work arrangement.

Most of the technical professionals with whom we spoke, however, have sought control of their time through true independent contracting. That is, they have set out on their own, effectively establishing their own businesses. As it turns out, there are several ways to use independent contracting as a way to reduce one's work hours.

At one extreme, we encountered a few individuals who contract with a single customer, generally an organization for which they once worked as employees. Most of these people, generally men, have retired from their previous jobs but continue to work a reduced schedule as a part-time contractor. Michael, an engineer who had worked for a large automobile manufacturer, took advantage of an opportunity to retire early, at age 53. He was quite happy to do so because he had become dissatisfied with changes in the company that, in his view, had placed accountants in charge of engineering functions and had brought in inexperienced college graduates who could not do the job at hand. His plan was to continue working after he retired, but he had no clear plans to become a contractor. A few weeks after retiring, however, Michael was approached by a contractor who offered him subcontracted work from his former employer. He decided to accept, established his own business (he even incorporated himself), and has worked as a contractor ever since, almost exclusively for his former employer. This arrangement does not give him much control over his hours; he estimates that he works about one-third of normal hours, but some weeks he works almost full-time, other weeks not at all. But since his motivation for working part-time is to "keep his hand in" while still having time to go fishing, erratic hours are not a problem for Michael. Indeed, he expresses considerable satisfaction in finding that his former employer still needs his knowledge to supplement the efforts of the new kinds of employees he so dislikes.

We encountered few nonretired individuals who work as contractors for a single customer. Jim, a computer scientist, is in this situation, but he has been doing it only six months, so it is hard to tell whether his relationship with a single employer will continue. He had been working for four years for a consulting firm when developments in his personal life forced him to make some changes: "Oh, I started getting divorced, and I have the children—two kids. They're with me, so I needed less time working and more time at home, so that's why I started working less hours. It was all right with the clients, but wasn't all right with them [his employer], because they required you to have forty billable hours a week, and I was probably doing thirty-two to thirty-five." Jim's solution was to shift from salaried status to contractor status, so that he was paid for the actual hours of work he performed. Jim anticipates doing some marketing in a couple of months and speculates about eventually becoming a broker for other contractors. It appears that he does not feel confident that his relationship with a single client will sustain him.

There are many reasons why contractors are most likely to have more than one client. Most employers contract out work that occurs sporadically, or that requires experience or expertise they do not have; if an organization has a permanent ongoing need, it makes sense to hire someone directly and solve the problem permanently. Most employees, even those who wish to work part-time, want to have sources of relatively steady, predictable work; relying on a single customer makes little sense, since few customers can guarantee a satisfactory flow of work. Finally, the IRS is increasingly skeptical of contracting arrangements between independent contractors and a single large organization, suspecting that such an arrangement is actually a concealed employment relationship. Many of the contractors with whom we spoke refer to the increasing scrutiny they are experiencing over this question; thus it is in their interest to be true contractors and have more than one client.

In fact, most of the contractors we interviewed do have multiple clients. Many technical writers, for example, work as independents, do considerable marketing work, and receive jobs from a wide variety of clients. Indeed, this seems to be the most common model for providing technical writing services in general; few employers have a consistent need for full-time technical writers. In both Chicago and Cleveland, there is an extensive network of independent technical writers—loosely organized through the Society for Technical Communication (STC)—who take advantage of the market for their services that this situation creates. Some of them are able to do so on a part-time basis by regulating the amount of work they accept.

Even a true contractor who has developed a more or less permanent relationship with a client typically supplements this assignment with work from other sources. Walt, an engineer, and Martin, a computer scientist, both have longstanding contracting relationships with an aluminum casting company. Martin works about 20 hours a week for this firm; Walt works for it somewhat more, approximately 100 to 150 hours a month. Both men see the aluminum company as their primary client and have worked for it for a long time: Walt for thirteen years, Martin for ten. Both, however, accept work from other clients. Neither is really considering severing connections with the aluminum company. At one point Walt became involved in a startup engineering firm, hoping that it might lead to something bigger, but he gave up on that undertaking years ago. Both he and Martin see work for other clients as supplementary to their main source of income, which is not quite adequate. And Martin acknowledges that he feels some pressure to do some marketing to "look more like a company than I do."

Why Contracting?

These variations in the organization of contracting are mirrored by variations in the paths by which part-timers become contractors. In some cases, becoming a part-timer coincides with becoming a contractor. This pattern is most typical of the agency-based contractors and of the retired contractors. For most independent contractors, however, the decision to become a contractor precedes the decision to work part-time. In these cases, contracting is not initially a solution to the problem of achieving part-time status; instead contracting proves compatible with part-time schedules for some of those who seek them.

At least two scenarios are typical among technical professionals who became contractors in order to become part-timers. Some respondents chose to become contractors because they had no other option. Sarah's employer refused to allow her to work part-time as a salaried employee. When Liz, a chemical engineer, approached her employer about part-time work after her son was born, they "couldn't figure out" what to do about benefits. She did not return to work after her maternity leave, but after a year, she said, she was going "stir crazy." Her previous job had taught her that technical writers had opportunities to work as independent consultants, so she reinvented herself (at least temporarily) as a technical writer and began taking on limited numbers of jobs. Her case is a particularly sharp illustration of a decision to become a contractor *in order to* work part-time.

For others, however, the decision to become a contractor is inextricably bound up with the decision to work part-time: both are desired outcomes; contracting is not simply a means to an end. Jane, a technical writer, told us that she had worked as a salaried employee, initially for a company making medical equipment. She found that she was not enjoying the work; she also went through a divorce. Marriage had been an obstacle to striking out on her own, since independent contracting often required her to work nights and weekends. Now, as a free agent, she feels able to do what she always wanted to do—become an independent. Jane has been working for several years as a self-employed technical writer, doing between 25 and 30 billable hours a week. While she sometimes works longer workweeks, she is clearly concerned to limit the amount of work she accepts. As she put it: "I don't want my whole life to be work; that's why I'm an independent." She told us of having been offered her dream job nine months into her career as an independent. She interviewed for the job, but she said, "When push came to shove, I couldn't do it. I did not want to get on that treadmill again." She prefers independence both because it allows her to work on projects she enjoys and because it allows her to keep work from dominating her existence.

Janine, a technical writer, is a more complex example of someone whose identity as a contractor is bound up with her desire to control her time. After graduating from college, she worked as a full-time contractor for a manufacturer of electronic controls. She worked on a contract basis because that was how one worked for that particular company, but she clearly saw herself as working for the firm, not as an independent contractor. After two years, she quit to have her first child. When she returned to work, she decided not to return to her previous employer, because she did not want full-time work; instead, she signed on with a small contracting firm that provided technical writing services to area companies. She worked for them for two years, three days a week, before she decided to strike out on her own. Her decision was based in part on her desire to maintain her part-time work schedule; although she had not experienced any direct pressure yet, Janine was aware that the firm had wanted her to work five days from the start, and saw her part-time status as temporary. Besides, she wanted to work at home now. As she put it:

> I always knew that I wanted to have children, and I wanted to find something that I thought was flexible enough to start out of my home, because I always knew that I wanted to be home with my children. So that was the main reason for quitting and becoming an independent. I had a hard time going back full-time, three days a week away from my child when I had just one, so for those years that I worked there, I cried. I didn't cry the morning I left there.

Many other contractors we interviewed had not started out with the intention to work part-time. Rather, they became contractors and then discovered, after their careers were well under way, that they wanted to reduce their work hours. They adapted their contracting to meet this newly discovered need.

Don, a computer scientist, embarked on a career as an independent consultant three years after finishing his master's degree. He had worked briefly for a defense contractor, but found that the environment was "too rigid," and he was troubled by the waves of layoffs that characterized the industry. He went to work instead as a salaried employee of a consulting firm. Almost immediately he was told that someone with his expertise could make two or three times more money as an independent, so he quit and became a contractor. His motivation had nothing at all to do with a desire to restrict his hours and everything to do with the entrepreneurial desire to be his own boss and make more money.

When we talked with Don, however, he had begun to rethink his approach to work. He referred to feeling "burned out" and to having grown dissatisfied with working 80 to 100 hours a week. He had cut back his work schedule to four days a week and speculated about his ability to reduce this schedule further to three. He talked about his desire to achieve some kind of balance, to make room for other activities. Don has come to view time as a resource that is as desirable as money. He feels, in fact, that he can have both: "I'm making now what I made five days a week last year. So what difference does it make? Better to have the time."

The Lessons of Gender

Although the correspondence is not absolute, we are struck by the fact that these various relationships between contracting and part-time work are associated with gender. To a great extent, it is female technical professionals who choose contracting as a way to achieve part-time work schedules; it is largely the men who are contractors first and then decide later to reduce their work hours. Since it was primarily among the contractors that we encountered male part-timers, it may be worth pausing to consider the significance of this apparent gender difference.

Most (although not all) of the female contractors decided to work part-time to accommodate their families. Jane, the technical writer and environmentalist, is an obvious exception. She is the only female contractor we met whose decision to work part-time was not related to family issues. All of the other female contractors we interviewed had sought part-time schedules because they wanted to spend time with their children or for other family reasons. One woman engineer we met had been a part-time contractor for much of her career because her husband, a physicist, had a disability that required her to be available to help him. Most of them, in other words, fit into the standard gendered model of the part-timer—a woman who reduces her hours to take care of others.

Just as very few men pursue part-time options for family reasons in organizations, it appears that few men pursue contracting primarily (or initially) for family reasons. It is probably significant that Jim, the computer scientist who became a contractor to accommodate his child care problems, did so after getting a divorce. In his situation, with custody of his children, he was *expected* to care for his children, since he had no female partner to do it for him. In effect, he resembles the female technical professionals who can justify working part-time (both to themselves and to others) as a reasonable way of doing what is expected of them.

The men tend to have one of two motivations for reshaping contracting as part-time work: either they are retiring after careers as full-time organizational professionals or they are scaling back, trying to avoid working such extremely long hours that work dominates their existence. Several of the male contractors, particularly those in the last group, see contracting as an alternative to organizational ways of doing things. In becoming contractors, they in effect have rejected certain aspects of the large organization. Rejecting organizational expectations about time, then, is simply an extension of a prior rejection of other standard assumptions about how one is supposed to work.

Several of the contractors resemble Don, the computer scientist. Like him, they are ambitious and had not initially sought reduced work schedules. Rather, they had seen contracting as a way to achieve a degree of independence. Don complains about the rigidity of the corporate environment in which he worked and refers repeatedly to his dislike of business politics. He identifies himself as a "rebellious kind of guy" who is uncomfortable with the subordination and infighting he encountered at work. His decision to work as a contractor is in part a decision to opt out of this way of doing things.

Others, like Martin, the computer scientist, conclude that they simply do not fit in the corporation. It is not so much that they are hostile to corporate practices; rather, they cannot function within them. Martin worked for several organizations in conventional jobs but had struggled with alcoholism and still identifies himself as a "newly recovered alcoholic." The travel that his earlier jobs involved presented real problems for him: "I had been traveling for too long and it's not a good way for a newly recovered alcoholic to start life again." Initially he looked for other kinds of conventional, salaried employment, but had little luck. When the opportunity to become a contractor presented itself, he recognized it as a better alternative for someone in his situation: "I kept looking for a permanent job, and kept not getting one. I think somebody was trying to tell me how to live life one day at a time."

Finally, a few are like Walt, the engineer: self-conscious rebels who explicitly reject the corporate world, both its organizational characteristics and its emphasis on making a lot of money. Like Martin, Walt had had several corporate jobs but did not like them: "I was always sort of the odd man out. I just didn't fit well in bureaucracies. I guess I always tried to do creative things when creative things weren't called for." He places his decision to become an independent contractor squarely in this context and sees it as a positive alternative to organizational ways of doing things: "I got away from bureaucracies. And I could directly do the work. I could do real work, as opposed to holding down a desk and just being part of an organization." To Walt, making a lot of money is not important; indeed, he told us that he doesn't have much respect for people who have made a fortune. Rather, he wants to do engineering, free of what he sees as bureaucratic interference; to him contracting is a way to become a really creative engineer.

Obviously, many men who become contract technical professionals never choose to reduce their work hours. It would be foolish, then, to argue that becoming a contractor because one dislikes aspects of the organizational world leads inevitably to a rejection of organizational expectations about time as well. Yet it is apparent that our male respondents had come to the idea of working less in the context of a preexisting desire to work differently. Moreover, it appears that virtually the only way for a man to reject organizational expectations about time is to become a contractor. While most female contractors and part-time employees focus primarily on the politics of organizational time, the male part-timers question the organizational world more generally.

The differences between male and female part-time technical professionals reflect the different realities they confront. The prime difference here may be that women have available to them a socially acceptable reason for opting out that men typically do not. Unless men are single parents, like Jim, the divorced computer scientist, it has traditionally been much more difficult for them to invoke family issues as a reason to reduce their work time. It is only when they opt out on other grounds ("I don't fit in," "I can't stand the bureaucracy," "I want to be independent") that the politics of time can be put back on the table.

Is Contracting the Answer?

Thus far, we have focused on how and why independent contracting becomes a vehicle for controlling and reducing work time for technical professionals. We must also ask whether contracting is a viable long-term strategy for creating part-time options. If independent contracting does become more common in technical fields, more technical people may consider it as a way to reduce their work hours. Whether contracting emerges as a more important way of doing so depends on two interrelated factors: how well it works for technical professionals and how willing employers are to accept the idea of contractors who work part-time.

One thing that might well deter technical professionals from becoming part-time contractors is a deterioration in their work. Since engineers, computer scientists, and technical writers all place a high value on doing varied, challenging work and on being treated as professionals who know what they are doing, the experience of being given only routine work or of being subjected to obtrusive supervision is likely to be unpleasant, even unacceptable. We originally suspected that being a part-timer, a part-time contractor in particular, would have these kinds of negative consequences. We expected to find, for example, that organizations would generally contract out only less desirable jobs, those that were relatively unimportant and uninteresting, particularly since contracting has traditionally thrived in the more routine areas of technical work. We are struck, therefore, by how seldom this is the case.

Once our independents decide to go solo, they find that their work is technically interesting and gives them a great deal of autonomy. These are good jobs. While a few people suspect they have been offered occasional jobs that are routine or unimportant, most are pleased with the variety and challenge of their work. Indeed, they stress that one of the advantages of contract work is the ability to avoid repetitive assignments and to choose what they agree to do. Janine, a technical writer, is typical. When we asked about the quality of the jobs she is offered, she replied:

> I turn down quite a bit of work, because that's one of the things I like, being out on my own, I like being able to pick and choose what I do. I want to be happy with what I'm doing and I can't be if I'm suffering on a project. I figure the money's not worth it to me, so I have turned down quite a bit. That doesn't seem to have hurt me thus far—at least, not that I know of, anyway.

Michael, the engineer who retired from a major automotive company and is now contracting on a part-time basis, echoes the sentiment: "I can pick and choose more. I can turn people down. I'll do it if it's an interesting project. But it has to be within my ability. I don't want to do something I've never done."

We did hear a few complaints about a decline in the quality of the work a part-time contractor is offered. Jackie is a technical writer who severely restricts her hours and works only at home, because she has a small child and has recently been diagnosed with cancer. She acknowledges, "It affects the assignments that I'm likely to be able to do, because I don't want to go on client site. So if there is bidding for a job that's client site, then I won't get it. So I'll end up with maybe another job that's not as challenging, or not as interesting, maybe, as one that might be on site. Then I miss out on meeting people, and that kind of thing." But Jackie also admits that this is not important to her at the moment, given her health problems, and she is aware that her situation is in large part the result of the unusually restrictive conditions she has placed on herself. Most contractors are not in this situation. They are able to get complex technical work of the same quality enjoyed by similar full-time, corporate technical staff.

Like many of the organizational employees we interviewed, part-time contractors are pleased about being liberated from what they see as the least desirable aspects of the job: meetings, politics, schmoozing. Although we heard occasional references to feelings of isolation, particularly from those who worked primarily at home, most seem to share Don's dislike of office politics. One of the attractions of contracting seems to be precisely the ability to get away from the complex social structure of organizational life, to be able to work in one's own way. Demands for one's physical presence are seen as particularly onerous. Ann, a technical writer, says:

> Normally, when I'm on site, there are certain hours they want you to be there. It's really like being at a regular job. You have a place where you sit. I like to say that I think my work hours are more productive at home than they are in the office. That's the one thing that kind of

really shook me up when I started working at home pretty consistently. I work with a higher intensity when I'm home, there's less standing around and shooting the breeze with people you know, to while away the slow minutes. One of the things, when you're on site, there's often a lot of down time. That makes me crazy, I just can't stand that. I can't stand sitting around with nothing to do.

"Why is there down time on site?" we asked.

Because you don't have a lot of ongoing job responsibilities. You might have a project that you're assigned to work on, but the project, the work might be out for review, or you're waiting for somebody to get you something. It's not like a normal job, where you have other things to go on with normally. And a lot of times they don't want you getting your hands in other things. A lot of times, people are a little protective of their turf. You're a bit of a threat to them.

Several people suggest that the pressure to be on site is at least partly the result of the poor work habits of their superiors. Janine argues that engineers want technical writers to work according to their schedules, schedules often dictated by their own lack of organization rather than the technical work itself: "Well, I'll tell you, I think a lot of it is that the engineers these days are so demanding. A lot of times they want to see you, to see what you're working on, they want to see the drawings right away, and it's almost more convenient if you're there one or two days a week, so that they can drop in."

Despite this kind of grumbling, many contractors spend substantial portions of their time working at home or in their own offices, an arrangement they clearly value. They experience demands to be on site as irritating interruptions of their normal way of working.

Part-time contractors also have considerable autonomy in how they do their work. The contracts they sign with their clients are not typically restrictive. Many contractors say they actually have to educate their clients about what they want, indicating that they are effectively in the driver's seat when it comes to establishing the parameters for the job.

On the other hand, deadlines are often less negotiable and more troublesome. They often have to decide up front whether they are willing to commit the hours to getting the job done to the client's schedule. At times a tight deadline creates real pressure to work longer hours than a part-timer wants to work. We heard many descriptions of working early in the morning or late at night to finish work that is due. These demands are complicated by the fact that most contractors have more than one job in process at a given time. Jane, a technical writer who has been working as a contractor since taking early retirement, explicitly avoids taking on more than one job at a time: "I prefer to work probably six to nine months out of the year. And I like to have my time. So I don't look for another job until the first job is out of the way." She frequently lets a month pass between projects. Most contractors cannot afford the gaps in work that Jane is willing to tolerate. Multiple projects entail multiple deadlines, and clients' demands can be unpredictable. Ann talks about how difficult it can be to juggle multiple projects:

> The trick is that you can't control the scheduling in a lot of these things even when you think you've got it scheduled, that this one's deadline is going to come in a week that you know the big project is going to be slow. But then this guy loses a week in review time. So then they're in even more of a hurry to get the finished product done. So you've got two big deadlines that fall in one week.

Of course, independents can turn down inconvenient jobs in a way not possible for their corporate counterparts. Doing so, however, may jeopardize one's ability to maintain a steady supply of work.

Managing the Amount of Work

Contractors' major difficulty in managing their time stems from their need to maintain a continuous and even flow of work. Sometimes they have more work than they can handle, but turning down a project may mean losing a potentially long-term client. At other times, they are short of work. Some report that they experience periods, sometimes lasting months, when little or no work is available. Such a hiatus obviously strains their economic resources and forces some of them to explore a return to salaried employment, to consider leaving the field, or to accept work they ordinarily would not consider.

The most dependable contracting arrangement, at least in the short term, is with a single client. In this kind of arrangement, it is usually possible for contractors to set their own hours and their own deadlines. They can estimate how long a job will take given their own particular working hours. Companies are most willing to contract in this way with former employees familiar with their technology and ways of operating. In particular, it is a way of retaining a valued employee who is threatening to leave altogether. Leonard, an independent computer consultant, describes how he arranged such a consulting arrangement: "I said I was going to retire. They said, 'Oh? We don't want to lose you. Have you considered staying?' I said no, not full-time, and not at market rates. So at that point we sat down and started discussing it."

As this description suggests, it is often employees nearing retirement who are comfortable with this form of contracting. Younger contractors are more likely to be wary of becoming dependent on a single customer, fearing that if the contract should end, they might have difficulty finding other jobs. Older workers may feel more secure in such arrangements, both because they do not anticipate continuing in the workforce indefinitely and because they know that the employer is highly dependent on their store of experience. Nonetheless, it is common for even younger contractors to make the transition to contracting by taking on a chunk of work from an old employer or a single client. This seems to be the path being taken by Jim, the divorced computer scientist.

Most contractors, however, report having multiple clients as a way of developing and sustaining an adequate supply of work. Acquiring a list of clients requires considerable effort that is not remunerated. Contractors report doing a lot of work simply generating business: making calls, going to professional meetings, and staying in contact with colleagues and former clients. Not all of them enjoy this kind of work, but most feel it is necessary:

> An aggressive person gets the work. You have to be a good salesperson. You also have to be a marketer. I'm bad at that. It's hard to do it when you don't have work. You're desperate and you don't want to sound like that when you call. When you're working, you don't feel

like it. They (whoever "they" are) say you should spend at least ten percent of your time on that.

An independent contractor who aims for a paid workweek of 25 hours may have to work more than that in order to get enough contracts.

Some of our respondents go further, implying that it is necessary to expand and even hire other practitioners to sustain a consulting practice over a prolonged period. Althea, a technical writer, has actually estimated the optimal number of clients she needs:

> You need a stable of clients—I think six is a comfortable number. I don't get work from all of them. I've got four right now. That way if you lose one, if management changes, if they say "no more contractors," you still have others. You can find another one. As a part-timer, it would be hard. You couldn't manage that many projects. I've been thinking about expanding for some time. For about a year I've been slightly overbooked. I'm having trouble making deadlines, squeaking by. I've got a contract that guarantees about twenty hours a week. That put me over the edge.

As Althea admits, maintaining a flow of business can create pressure to do too much or to expand. One way to grow while maintaining control over one's time is described by Tony, another technical writer. By establishing a company that employs eight other technical writers, he has been able to reduce his workweek to around 30 hours. To do so, however, he has to spend virtually all his time doing sales and marketing work, leaving the actual technical writing to his employees. Even he reports down periods when he has to work longer hours on jobs he would not take in prosperous times.

Michael, the engineering contractor, insists, "The only way to control it is to say no." But contractors often cannot afford to refuse work because they fear the permanent loss of a client, or they fear they will antagonize a good client by delaying the completion of a project. They dread being forced into periods of full-time activity or experiencing long periods with inadequate income.

Some contractors have worked out a solution: they belong to a network that allows them to even out the workload. They maintain contact with other practitioners in the field, former clients, former employers, and others who may be sources of information about possible contracts. Professional associations also serve as a more formal kind of network for practitioners. The Society for Technical Communication (STC) serves as a clearinghouse for information on projects for technical writers and a venue in which they can meet one another and perhaps potential clients.

The existence of such networks allows contractors to reduce the laborious work of locating business. A contractor may get a call from someone in her network informing her of an opportunity, or may search for work by contacting individuals within her network. Almost all of the independent contractors we interviewed said that they get most of their work through colleagues and former clients, although some feel that cold calls are still necessary to maintain a successful consulting business.

What is more, networks facilitate subcontracting arrangements. A contractor confronted by a surplus of work can avoid losing valuable clients by accepting too much work and contracting out some or all of it to others in his network. Subcontracting tends to spread the wealth around, and it helps practitioners who lack a strong client base of their own to find work when they need it. Of course, no network can help if there is an area-wide decrease in the demand for technical services.

It is possible to exaggerate the importance of these networks. For obvious reasons, contractors are sometimes reluctant to share clients with one another. Jane admits to being a bit secretive about her clients:

> If I get work through STC, it's through the membership bulletin. But otherwise, I have had people call and tell me they have found my name on the STC, but not referrals. Part of that, I think, and I'm guilty of that too, we're a little uncomfortable sharing our clients. When we have a meeting, somebody will say, "I have a client that has this many employees in this industry, pharmaceuticals or health care," but nobody says who it is. I mean, we're all just real quiet about that. But you have to be. It's a competitive business. And it's a business. And because it's also new, we have ethics about how we treat our clients, but I have not seen anything on how we treat each other.

In a competitive business, it can be dangerous to be too cooperative.

There are also risks associated with subcontracting. Tony, the successful technical writing contractor who employs other technical writers, notes that he has to take care to ensure the quality of the work done by subcontractors. Since personal reputation is crucial to getting business, he feels at risk whenever he farms out work. He has developed a series of worksheets and checklists that he uses in an effort to control his subcontractors. As he puts it, "You need to find people who are good enough so that they won't cost you business." Despite these dangers, formal and informal networks remain an efficient way of managing time.

There are also more formal responses to the uneven distribution of contracting work. One strategy is to join forces with a small number of other practitioners. Ian, a computer consultant, says the advantage of such groups is that "you're able to pool your money. Somebody can be down for some period of time, and that would not be a problem."

Obtaining work through contract houses, organizations that contract with clients and then subcontract work to independents, is another possibility. Jane has mixed emotions about this strategy:

> It's two-sided. One is, when you're working for yourself, you have all the risk, so you earn more money. You're the one negotiating the contract, dealing with "Are they happy?" When you subcontract, you're just an employee. All the ugliness, if there is any, doesn't touch you. It doesn't matter, unless they don't want you to come back, but I've never had that. So I'm a lot freer to just concentrate on the writing, I don't have to worry about is this bill going to be paid? All that kind of thing.

Ann, another technical writer, has reservations about the quality of the work she can get in this way:

> It's not usually great work. I have a lot of experience, and a lot of these people, we call them body shops in the business, they just want warm bodies in chairs. And how well you can do the work is not a concern to them. But the contract houses, a lot of them don't even understand what it is we do. A lot of them place writers as a sideline business to placing engineers and programmers. They haven't a clue what the

client really needs. And it's just not the way, not the work I want to be doing over the long haul. I want more challenging work at this point in my career. I mean, yeah, I sit there sometimes and go, "There's an easier way to live. You could just go do this on-site work and you know they pay thirty-five bucks an hour and you'd get closer to two thousand hours a year. And you'd be sittin' pretty." But I can't live that way.

Contract houses provide income that is more regular but they may pay less and limit independents' ability to control the kind of work they do.

Most of the contractors with whom we spoke have developed reasonably effective ways of regulating work flow and making their work time fit acceptably with the other aspects of their lives. Moreover, one can imagine ways in which this control could be extended. Restriction of entry to a profession, for example, could reduce the competitiveness of the field and encourage more exchange of information and subcontracting. Or more reciprocal long-term relationships could develop among large firms, contractors, and subcontractors. Some observers claim to have seen precedents in Japanese business practice and in the Italian industrial regions (Harrison 1994, Piore and Sabel 1984). Were this practice to develop, many of the problems of uncertain, erratic supplies of work and income might be overcome. Overall, controlling the flow of work, while often difficult, is not an insuperable obstacle to sustaining part-time work on a contract basis.

Regulating the Work

The other factor on which the future growth of part-time contracting depends is the attitude of employers. As with part-time work generally, employers may be reluctant to accept part-time contracting since it deviates from the work practices to which they are accustomed. The perceived problems of managing part-time technical professionals are magnified when the part-timers are contractors. Not only are these technical professionals released from the time structure of the organization, they are also beyond the reach of the standard rewards used to ensure loyalty and exert control over educated labor.

The standard career package for corporate professionals—professional training, long-term careers, extended job contracts—developed initially to ensure the loyalty of employees doing important and highly discretionary work. It is because of the difficulties of regulating complicated technical work by market mechanisms that contracting has traditionally been thought of as suitable only for the most routine and least skilled of professional technical work, such as drafting. These conditions clearly do not apply to the people we interviewed. Their work is as complex and autonomous as that of any corporate employee. How, then, is their work regulated? If contracting is to continue to play a significant part in expanding the options of technical professionals, this question is worth exploring.

The most convenient way for employers to ensure that they get good reliable workers is to contract with people who have already demonstrated their reliability by working as corporate employees full-time. This is a very common route for persons preparing for retirement. Many other contractors set up on their own to acquire employment that is more flexible but continue to do a lot of work for their former employers, who already know them. In some organizations, becoming a contractor is the only way an established employee is allowed to work part-time.

These are the easy decisions. In these cases, employers have well-established reputations on which to rely. How do they handle working with people with whom they have no such relationships? In part, they can rely on the market to coerce contractors to do their best, since they know their survival depends on their ability to find new clients. Virtually every contractor with whom we spoke talked about their vulnerability to clients' judgments of them and their work. As Jane put it, "Because I'm a freelancer and the way I operate, the way all of us operate, if they don't like us or they don't think we can do the job, at any moment they can say, 'Don't come back tomorrow.'" Since these statements usually came in response to inquiries about how clients control contractors, contractors clearly understand that the market is operating as an impersonal form of control.

Employers, however, obviously prefer to avoid trial and error in the market. They would rather select individuals on whom they can count to do a good job the first time. Here again, the social structure of ostensibly impersonal market relationships becomes apparent, as respondents emphasize the importance of networks and reputation to success as a contractor. We have already noted that many contractors build up relationships with future clients before they leave organizational employment, and contractors generally agree that the keys to getting business are being known and having a reputation. The result is that contractors place far more emphasis on networking and contacts than on advertising or cold calls as a way of getting business (although many do advertise and make cold calls on occasion, particularly when things are slow). We heard innumerable stories about how jobs just fell into contractors' laps, how a person with whom they'd worked in the past called them to offer a project or suggested they call someone else. Tom, a computer scientist, is particularly emphatic in his belief in the importance of networking: "Networking is just it. There is no substitute. There's no alternative. You can't network, forget it, from my point of view, and I've never heard anything different."

When clients are reasonably familiar with an individual contractor or have heard good reports of him, they have a relatively high level of trust in that contractor's ability and willingness to do what they want. This is what some organizational theorists (Lewicki and Bunker 1995) have referred to as "knowledge-based trust." In these circumstances, their inability to control directly what the contractor does becomes less of an issue. Janine makes the connection between autonomy and reputation explicit: "I usually beat the deadlines. They don't really keep tabs, I guess, because I've sort of become known for beating the deadlines." As in many other freelance occupations, reputation is carried by word of mouth, and references and portfolios become important factors in establishing working relationships.

An alternative to a personal relationship is a highly specific contract that dictates how, when, and where the work will be done. Such contracts seem to be rare. Technical contractors typically do have some kind of written contractual arrangement with their client/employer, although this is not the practice among the contractors we met who work for a single company. Ordinarily, upon learning of a potential contract, they bid on the job, and if they are successful, they enter into a written agreement specifying deadlines, expected outcomes, and the like. We are struck, however, by the influence contractors feel they have over the content of these contracts, and by the high level of autonomy such contracts typically allow contractors. Thus Janine, the technical writer:

> I think a lot of freelancers—I don't know this for sure—try to act like they work for the company— which I do, in a sense, but it's my own company, so I try to run it as a company rather than me freelancing for them. That's why I went off on my own, because I want them to consider me as a company, and not have to feel they can put deadlines and pressures on me.

Althea, another technical writer, experiences considerable variety in the type of contracts she signs, adding that clients are often not particularly knowledgeable about what they want, so that the contractor has to be proactive: "I start writing. I do installation: how to install, weight issues, access to the insides, visibility of LED displays (you can only see them from certain angles). I have to figure this out; the engineers don't tell you."

Some contracts are quite specific about how the work needs to be done, especially in those infrequent cases in which a company has a standard format for its products; working for the government is often cited in this respect. In such cases, companies often specify review procedures and build milestones into contracts. A review can be a battle, and the company typically wins. It is equally common, however, for respondents to see reviews as "not a problem." Whether or not milestones are included in the contract varies considerably, and several respondents, like Ben, an engineer, indicate that they insist on milestones themselves for their own reasons:

> Q. Have they typically had review points or milestones or anything like that built into them? You've had one that was long enough that that might have been a reasonable expectation.
> A. More so ones that I've put in, because these other people didn't have the management sense that I had. Having been through a large company and seen some of the structure that they put on top of the projects, so the managers can get a handle on them, he hasn't been through that, and doesn't have that kind of rigor, and it shows in other things that he does.

Q. You're putting this in for your protection, or for his?
A. My own sense of accomplishment. To feel like I am getting something done—so I can say, "OK, I spent a week working on something. What do I have to show for it?" I'm going to give him a bill for this past month, I want to have something to show him that this is actually done, at the same time I give him the bill, so he has some sense that he's getting some value for his money.[1]

Overall, the general impression is of flexible negotiation processes resulting in relatively open-ended contracts that allow considerable autonomy. Martin, the computer consultant, concluded: "I think that I have more autonomy—certainly more autonomy than somebody in house would have."

Employers rely strongly on the professionalism of contractors. An important component of all kinds of technical training is its incorporation of corporate values that are internalized by professionals. These values become their own ideology of professionalism, ensuring that they do work of the kind the employer demands, even when they could choose to do otherwise (Whalley 1986). Technical contractors have strong professional attitudes that motivate them to work hard, complete work promptly, and be responsive to clients. Technical practitioners tend to be committed to technical work per se and can frame their efforts on behalf of employers as "doing a good job" and "getting the technology right." According to Martin:

You have to do things like getting on the Web and things like that. Some of these things, frankly, eventually result in increasing your skills, or increasing your value to your clients. I know, quite frankly, the fact that I am on CompuServe, and there regularly, has made differences. Getting different drivers, for example, printer drivers for other people around there. In a sense I provide a service to them that they wouldn't have otherwise. I print their barcode labels for them, partly because they don't want to do it themselves.

Q. So there's a certain amount of that kind of work that is not formally paid for but it makes you do the rest of your job better?

---

1. Ben's comment that billable hours can have the effect of validating what the contractor has been doing sounds very much like Elaine Yakura's (2001) finding that billables are both an overt measure of performance and a legitimization of the value of a contractor's services.

A. Yeah, actually, some of the stuff I do kind of as a hobby. I think people who are really into data processing—the people who are at the top—they have data processing as a hobby too. In some ways, it amazes me when I hear of data processing managers that don't have a home computer. They do exist, but I'm surprised.

Many of our respondents also talk about their feelings of responsibility and loyalty to the companies or individuals with whom they contract. Martin adds that personal loyalties are at least as important:

Well, it's been said that people in data processing have more loyalty to the field than they do to the company that they're with, and I guess, generally speaking, I like to do a professional, generally good job. But I feel a pretty big responsibility to the people that I've been working for—not to, essentially, leave them in the lurch.

Althea adds that there is a considerable degree of self-interest implicit in this attitude. When we asked why she exerts herself to do a good job for clients, she said: "I want them to stay in business." She laughed. "There are a couple of reasons. I had clients who didn't want me to do as good a job as I did. I want to do a good job; I don't want someone to look at something I did and say, 'Who did this?'"

Technical consultants demonstrate the interpersonal dimensions of contractual relationships (Granovetter 1985). They are strongly motivated by a combination of loyalty to technology itself, to individuals, to employers, and to their own sense of identity with their product.

For our respondents, independent contracting proves a viable way of getting control over working time. While there are difficulties, particularly in the management of work flow, most seem able to work around these difficulties and to develop satisfactory part-time arrangements as contractors. The proliferation of contractors has forced organizations to develop new ways of managing technical professionals, and part-time contractors do not seem to pose any special problems for them.

Does Independence Equal Flexibility?

Questions remain, however. Is independent contracting an inherently more flexible way of gaining control over work time? Why do some technical professionals choose contracting as a way of achieving control over their time instead of remaining in an organizational context? There are clearly certain obvious differences between the contractors and corporate professionals. Occupation obviously makes a difference. Technical writing has a long history of contracting, while engineering is more organization-based, so that most of the part-time technical writers but only a few of the engineers we met were contractors. It was also noticeable that most of the part-time men we interviewed were contractors, while women were more evenly distributed across the two groups. Related to this last point, the range of motivations for seeking part-time work was broader among the contractors. For organizational professionals, the dominant motivation was children; for contractors, this was only one among a variety of motivating factors about which we heard.

These differences, however, do not imply that certain people who want to work part-time will inevitably gravitate toward contracting, while others with different characteristics will choose to remain within organizations. Rather, they reflect the reality that organizations dictate who may and who may not seek part-time work inside the corporate world. The prevailing corporate view is that motherhood is the most widely acceptable reason for seeking part-time status. Flexible work policies are usually described as "family friendly," which usually means "female friendly." One result is that many organizational employees, particularly men, who have an interest in customizing their work arrangements have no choice but to become contractors. If corporations changed their approach, perhaps some of the men who tell survey researchers that they want to reduce their hours and spend more time with their kids will follow women into part-time employee status. It is also likely that corporate employees will seek part-time status for a greater range of reasons. The predominance of contractors among part-time technical writers also reflects a corporate rather than an individual choice, since contractors predominate among technical writers generally as a result of corporate outsourcing practices. Were this situation to change, it is likely that the situation of part-time technical writers would change along with it.

One difference between contractors and employees, however, appears to have little to do with organizational practices per se. Many of the male contractors we encountered became contractors *before* they became interested in working part-time, while only a very few women had made their work choices in this order. Here we can only speculate. It may be that women who don't fit in the corporate world—in the way that Walt, the contract engineer, did not—have historically had another option for constructing an identity— motherhood. If they don't like the corporate rat race, they can quit and become full-time parents, an option unavailable to men, since fatherhood is not defined as an all-encompassing identity. As more women struggle to construct lives built around multiple identities, however, the motherhood default may become less attractive; in that case, more female analogues to Walt may appear. Perhaps the difference is simply a matter of history. Women are far less numerous than men in the technical professions, and as a group they have been working in these fields for less time than men. As technical roles become more common for women and as the women who do this kind of work become more diverse, the difference between male and female contractors may begin to diminish.

The relative absence of stable differences between part-time contractors and corporate employees suggests that moves from independent to corporate status and back again will be considered simply the normal choices that make up the constructed careers of professionals who seek flexibility in work. At the moment, these choices are limited by corporate policies and practices. The people we met are making choices, within these limits, as a way of maximizing opportunities at a particular point in the life course.

In light of what we heard from part-time technical professionals, it is reasonable to assume that contracting will grow rather than shrink in the future. In occupations such as technical writing, contracting is already an established way of conducting business. It is quite likely that technical writers who want to work part-time will pursue this option through contracting. Organizational careers remain much more common in computer science and particularly in engineering. As our respondents made clear, however, the boundary between an in-house employee working on a project team and an in-dependent contractor is becoming blurred. At the end of a project, corporate employees often have to bid for jobs in other sectors of the company with no guarantee of acceptance. As corporations develop flatter hierarchies, there are signs of a growing occupationalization of technical work. Technical expertise is increasingly transferable between companies, and high levels of specific expertise become valuable to companies only for specific projects. The lifetime employment and extended career ladders of the past are rapidly becoming obsolete. For this reason, the traditional distinction between a majority of permanent employees and a floating minority of temporary contractors is diminishing. Using contracting as a means of acquiring control of one's work schedule is becoming increasingly feasible as long-term opportunity costs decline.

We are nonetheless wary of the chorus of voices hailing independent contracting as the wave of the future, or of predicting that independent contracting will become the normal way to develop a part-time work schedule. Conversations with contractors about their own future plans produced a variety of responses. Many do talk about liking to work as contractors and being able to reduce their hours this way. Many admitted they could not imagine going back to the corporate world. Even people who have opted for contract work only because they had no other means of reducing their work hours feel that way. Several respondents, however, do envisage returning to full-time work, either as contractors or in organizations. Many of them point to the problems of managing their time and to the economic constraints imposed by part-time contracting. Still others talk about expanding their businesses, becoming agents or brokers for other technical professionals, speculating that in the long run, this is the only really viable way to make a good living as a contractor working a reasonable number of hours. A small number of our respondents have actually succeeded in moving in this direction. Most of the people who speculate about taking this course, however, admit they have not yet made any concrete plans. Thus we cannot say for certain that contracting provides a viable mechanism for long-term part-time work. Many of our respondents appear to be in some doubt about whether their present arrangements are stable. Lacking the ability to look into the future, we can only note these doubts as reasons for caution.

Nonetheless, particularly for those who find it difficult to secure part-time work, perhaps because of cultural resistance to male corporate part-timers or simply managers' obduracy, contracting provides an additional choice, a possibility of really customizing hours of work without sacrificing the qualities of work that make technical professions so often satisfying to their practitioners. In fact, what characterizes our respondents more than anything else is this insistence on being able to continue to make choices about their work lives as their careers and their life course progress. They are not content to remain locked into a rigid professional career track; instead they explore lateral moves in organizations and even across occupational boundaries. They are willing to turn their backs on corporate careers and try being independent if that seems better suited to their needs; they are equally willing to return to the corporate world if contracting doesn't work out or if their needs change. Just as they do not wish to be entirely defined by their work, neither do they want to accept permanently a status conferred upon them by their current employment arrangements.

6

"I'm a Mom, Not a Housewife"

For many of the people we talked with, especially the working mothers, arranging to customize work time is only the first step in putting work in its place. The workplace is not the only institution that is so greedy of time that it can create an all-defining identity if it is allowed to. Indeed, during the 1950s it was the family that did just that for most middle-class American women. Being a housewife wasn't a job in the sense we talked about earlier, it was a career—a definer of identity and a total absorber of time. To make space in their lives for other things, working moms—indeed, all parents who work for pay—need to customize their home time too. If the norm of market work is the full-time male worker supported by a full-time wife at home, the norm of family work is the full-time housewife supported by a full-time breadwinner. As a generation of feminist research has pointed out, schools, traditional eating patterns, middle-class standards of household cleanliness, and the growing pressure for the active involvement of parents in all aspects of child rearing, from conception to college graduation, all assume that there is a full-time mom at home to do the work.[1] If parents want to pursue a dual commitment to work and parenting, somehow both these traditional patterns need to be reconstructed.

Most conventional jobs do not automatically provide profession-

---

1. The literature on this subject is extensive, but for especially useful insights see DeVault 1994, Smith 1987, Williams 2000, and Hochschild 1989.

als with interesting, rewarding work and at the same time enable them to control and limit the time they devote to paid work. Nonetheless, most of the professionals with whom we spoke *had* been able, at least in the short term, to reconstruct work with these objectives in mind. But what of their experiences at home? The demands of home life can be just as greedy and unforgiving as the demands of work. Just as conventional work can prevent the enjoyment of domestic life, the time demands of conventional domestic life can make the enjoyment of work problematic. To achieve the combination of satisfying work and satisfying lives away from work that our respondents sought, it is equally necessary to restructure home time, particularly when the home includes children.

It Works Out Well

Parenthood drew many of the people with whom we spoke into part-time work. Moreover, these professionals speak of parenting not as a chore from which they cannot escape but as a positive value, something they enjoy and see as rewarding. Simply grafting the conventional housewife's role onto part-time work will not do for our respondents, who are looking for a rewarding experience at home, not the drudgery and oppression characteristic of domesticity. We must ask, therefore, how gratifying part-time technical professionals find their experiences at home.

Most of the people with whom we spoke reported that their decision to work part-time has had positive consequences at home. Despite inevitable problems and complaints, our respondents appear to be quite satisfied with their domestic lives and pleased with the effect the change has had on their relationships with their children and other members of their families.

Meredith, a computer scientist who works as a contractor in the telecommunications industry, did not plan to switch to part-time work. In fact, she worked full-time after her two children (now aged six and nine) were born. Eventually, however, she found that she was "going crazy" and decided to reduce her hours. She considered quitting altogether, but felt that her family could not afford the loss of income (her husband was starting a new business and was bringing in little or no money), and in any case, she values work too much as a source of social contact, a sense of accomplishment, and self-confidence. When we spoke with her, she had been working about 30 hours a week for a year and a half. Like many of the people with whom we spoke, she describes her current situation as ideal because it provides her with real flexibility: "I'm kind of in utopia here. I can work from home if I need to, by dialing in to the computer. I specifically choose my own hours, and I can work four hours today and eight hours tomorrow, as long as I do my thirty hours." What does she use the flexibility for? Meredith told us that she devotes most of the additional time to her kids, doing things with them, being involved in their activities. She describes the advantages of her new arrangements this way:

> This is great. I find myself complaining some days, and I think, "Wait a minute. This really did what I wanted it to." I'm able to do the Cub Scouts, the PTA stuff, and I'm able to be involved in their lives, to be able to get them where they need to go or want to go. Last year, when my son was in kindergarten, every three weeks I would volunteer in their classroom—they were half day. That was really great to be able to do. That was really nice. I think—they're little kids so they don't appreciate anything—but I think they notice. They know that I'm involved and they like seeing me at school, and having the teachers and principal know me. It's important to them.

Like many of the parents, Meredith expresses a sense of achievement, of having been able to accomplish something worthwhile because of the flexibility her work schedule allows her. Her satisfaction goes beyond the kind of externally imposed need to engage in symbolic parenting described by Anita Garey (1999). She has not gotten involved in the Cub Scouts and the PTA because she wants to show others that she is a good mother, or even to convince herself that she is. Meredith's orientation is to her children, not to other mothers, and she finds her experiences with them to be fulfilling.

Sarah, the part-time chemical engineer who works as a "tied" contractor, goes even further. Like Meredith, she complains that working full-time had been a tremendous source of stress. Part of the problem is that it prevents her from enjoying her work:

Because you had full-time work or more than full-time work, and you needed to go pick somebody up or somebody gets sick at school, or somebody gets hurt, and it's much easier to accommodate those things now. I just found myself sometimes where, really, I needed to go spend a week somewhere to work on this project and I didn't want to do it. I couldn't feel good about getting my work done when I didn't want to go and do what needed to be done to get it done.

Part-time work enables Sarah to enjoy her work more because she doesn't experience this kind of conflict. She also likes part-time work because she finds positive experiences at home.

I like the part-time arrangement. I have to say I really enjoy going to the bus stop with the kids. I didn't do that before, I had to drop them at day care, because we had to leave early in order to be downtown. It didn't work. I remember being devastated when my son started kindergarten. I couldn't put him on the bus down at the corner. My husband thought that was so funny, he's like "What's the big deal?" To him that wasn't important, but those things were to me, so when I took my daughter to the bus last year, and we and the dog go down every morning and wait for the bus, I just really enjoy having the opportunity to do that. My son, when he was in fifth grade, last year, he said, "Don't go to the bus stop with me on the first day of school." I said, "Look, I quit my job to go to the bus, I'm going down to the bus!" We all laughed. "I have to go to the bus stop; this is something I have to do. I don't care if you want me to go."

What is particularly significant about this anecdote is Sarah's delight in her arrangements because of the personal satisfaction they bring her. She finds that she enjoys doing things like this, that they are satisfying to her. She even confesses to having guilt feelings about working part-time: "I could be out working full-time, am I being selfish to my family?" Sarah feels a degree of compulsion to work full-time, to contribute more economically to her household. Thus for her working part-time is not something she feels compelled to do by external pressure. On the contrary, it is something she does because she finds it allows her a greater degree of personal fulfillment, both at work and at home.

Managing Domestic Labor

Meredith and Sarah exemplify all of our respondents who are parents: all said that being with the kids is a positive source of identity and pleasure for them and that part-time work facilitates their enjoyment of it. The same, however, cannot be said about domestic chores. These are not a source of great satisfaction for any of these technical professionals. They think very differently about chores than they do about child care. Chores are not interesting or stimulating. We met no closet Martha Stewarts.

One frequently mentioned risk of working part-time is that it threatens to rigidify traditional gender roles, to cause the person who spends more time at home (usually the mother) to do the lion's share of domestic labor. In that case, housework might jeopardize the gains anticipated by those who choose to work part-time. An expansion of this kind of work would eat into time that could be devoted to truly gratifying activities (paid work, being with one's kids). Thus we must ask how our respondents deal with domestic chores. Does domestic labor prevent part-time technical professionals from reaping the benefits of their reduced work hours?

I'm Not a Housewife

Part-time technical professionals tend to live in unequal households. They are not, for the most part, examples of the "shared parenting" arrangements described by Francine Deutsch (1999). Yet, despite some grumbling, few of them regard these unequal arrangements as a major problem. How can we explain their acceptance of this situation? Partly it is a matter of their ability to explain to themselves why it is OK for them to do the lion's share of domestic labor. Partly it is a matter of having the resources to reduce the burden they have to bear. Most important, it is a matter of their approach to domestic labor. They neither place a great deal of emphasis on it nor spend an enormous amount of time or energy on it. Domestic labor is unequally shared, true, but the pie that is being divided unequally is small enough so that the problems are also small. Our respondents do not find that housework prevents them from enjoying either their paid work or their domestic lives.

We encountered almost no part-time technical professionals for whom domestic labor was a priority. They do not talk about cooking, cleaning, and doing laundry in the same way they talk about paid labor or child care. They do not express regret, for example, about their inability to bake pies or maintain a clean house. Nor do they talk about chores as important items that needed to be balanced with the other activities that form part of their lives. When they talk about "going crazy" as full-time workers, it is about their inability to combine their work activities with their need and desire to be with and care for their families. Chores are to be ignored or to be got out of the way. Indeed, one of the advantages of working part-time is being able to get chores done before the weekend or the evening to create family time together, free of errands and cleaning. "I like to get all the shopping and the cleaning done during the week. That's what's good about part-time. It frees up the evenings and weekends for family time when we can both be together with the kids." Ellen, a part-time engineer, makes a very similar statement:

> I can get the grass cut during the week and then we can play on the weekends. You know, it's like you don't have to do all the chores on the weekend. And my in-laws have a summer home in Michigan, on the lake, so that I can get everything ready and we can take off for the weekend. I think if I was working full-time, we wouldn't be able to do that.

Because chores are things to be got out of the way in order to free up time for other things, they try to limit the amount of time they spend on them. Family sociologists note that as more and more women enter the labor force, they tend to reduce the amount of time they spend on domestic labor. Our respondents are very much part of this trend. When we asked Linda, a part-time environmental engineer, whether she felt compelled to maintain a high standard of order and cleanliness, she responded, "I don't worry about that sort of thing—a messy living room doesn't bother me. There's just not that many tasks." Beth, one of the part-time engineers who works as a tied contractor, says that for a while she tried to cook meals the day before so that a "good" meal was always available; but she found cooking at night "discouraging," so she changed her approach:

I guess I usually cook maybe three or four meals a week. It used to be that I cooked a certain amount and it would be two meals, but we can't do that anymore. There's usually just a little bit left. So whenever I see that there are enough little bits of something left, we just have a day of leftovers. Tom enjoys cooking. I don't really enjoy it, because I really never have time to do it. My aunt who is a chemist says that it's too much like chemistry [laughs]. You've been doing chemistry all day; you don't want to do it when you get home. But we do simple things, quick things.

Thus Beth demonstrates how many part-timers limit the amount of domestic labor they do, even avoiding it altogether at times. Alice, another engineer, makes explicit this general view of domestic labor: "My major reason for going part-time was to be with the kids, not to clean. I make that a priority. I do have to fight off the domestic chores sometimes. When the kids take a nap—they both nap—do I clean or read a magazine?"

Financial Resources

By deemphasizing and limiting domestic labor, part-time technical professionals are able to limit its interference with the things they really want to do. But there are also other factors that help them get a life: they have access to a variety of resources for dealing with the demands of domestic labor.

The most important factor, and the one that most distinguishes the people we talked with from the vast majority of part-time employees, is that they earn enough to lighten the load. They belong to an affluent class of corporate professionals. Almost all had been well paid as full-time workers, in some cases earning salaries that reached six figures. Even as part-time workers many were earning $35,000 or more, so that their personal incomes were actually above the average household income for the period during which we were interviewing.

Further, whether or not they are able to earn high incomes as part-timers, virtually all of our respondents have spouses whose incomes are also relatively high. Their marriages to professionals and corporate managers place them in the upper tier of U.S. household incomes. With one or two exceptions, household incomes for the part-timers we interviewed exceed $60,000; many have household incomes in excess of $100,000. Almost no one responded to our questions about the economic effects of reducing work hours by mentioning hardship or belt-tightening.

As important as the salaries are the benefits. Some of our corporate part-timers are fortunate enough to belong to progressive companies that offer benefits to part-time staff. Ellen, for example, explained that she worked 25 hours a week because that is the cut-off point for eligibility for benefits. Even as a part-timer she is eligible for full benefits with prorated paid vacations. Sometimes the prorating of benefits becomes quite complex. Jennifer and Lisa, the engineers working for a defense contractor, were amused to find that among the benefits that are prorated by their employer are personal days for deaths in the family. They joked, resentfully, that part-timers are supposed to "grieve less."

Like most part-timers in the United States, however, many of our respondents lost access to some or all employer-provided benefits when they switched to part-time work, either because they shifted to independent contractor status or because their employer's policies extended full benefits only to full-time employees. For many Americans, given the absence of comprehensive national insurance programs, this loss would be a major reason to remain at work full-time. Since most of those with whom we spoke have access to benefits through their spouses, however, that problem does not affect them. Independent contractors who do not have a spousal benefit plan usually earn enough to purchase benefits through a professional association or other local network. Even Meredith, whose household is struggling financially because she is a part-time contractor and her husband is embarking on a new career of self-employment, said that they have been able to purchase comprehensive medical and dental insurance and a life insurance policy on their combined incomes.

The combination of high family incomes and good benefits places this group in a class that is legitimately free to ignore many of the real economic penalties experienced by other part-time workers. In fact, most, though not all, are free to be full-time homemakers should they wish. Thus professionals like Liz can hire someone else to do some of the domestic work they would otherwise have to do themselves:

Well, as I guess you can tell [looking around her], we don't exactly do much cleaning around here. We have a team that comes in to do the big stuff every couple of weeks, but my husband certainly didn't marry me to look after the house. We worked too hard before we had kids to bother very much about cleaning and cooking and stuff, and we haven't changed much. I guess I spend more time cooking than I used to. It's not always so easy to eat out as much as it used to be, but he still brings home takeout once a week.

Many of our respondents either make use of or are considering hiring household cleaning help. Having a cleaner is obviously quite important to them. As Meredith said about her cleaner, "She will be the last thing I give up!"

Others pay for a variety of services. One of the more common is baby-sitting. On the days when they are at work, a number of our respondents hire someone either to stay at their house and watch their children or to provide some form of in-home day care. Ellen, who works three days a week, has been able to locate a college student who attends school three days a week and whose free days coincide with two of Ellen's workdays. Some also pay for part-time institutional day care, although, as we have seen, many prefer alternative forms of child care.

Partial Commodification

The part-timers we encountered, thus, are willing to engage in a kind of partial commodification of domestic labor, contracting out portions of it as a way of reducing the need to do it themselves. As affluent professionals, they are in an economic position to do so. However, they also have other resources on which they can draw. Even if they are unwilling to buy domestic services, they can reduce their burden in other ways.

First, they do share some of the work with their spouses. Some women said their husbands do the cooking, or like to do laundry, or perform this or that domestic chore. While real domestic equality is rare, as we shall see, many can identify a few tasks that their spouse performs. Particularly when it comes to the mundane aspects of looking after children (getting them ready for school, washing them, etc.), many husbands seem willing to do the work. A few husbands share the parenting, but this arrangement requires the husband to have a flexible schedule as well. John is an engineer now employed part-time by a major national electronic corporation, who had been employed as a full-time technical manager; his wife, also an engineer, is employed by the same company. When their first child was born, she arranged a part-time job for herself. He found this arrangement unsatisfactory, especially after subsequent children were born:

> Well, it was OK, it just seemed like the amount of time I would have with the kids was kind of short. I got home at six-thirty and with them having to be in bed at eight, it just seemed short. And then with the third, the numbers would go down, the amount of time would just go down. Of course, we are not good at spending money. We didn't need to have one and a half times a person's income. We didn't need it. And so if you're not spending more, and you don't need to do that, then why do that? So there seemed to be good reasons not to. We don't both need to go crazy being at home all day with the kids, we could both have a professional life, and so it seemed like a winning situation.

Thus John and his wife have found a way to reconcile commitment to work and commitment to family. He talks about himself as having changed, having moved away from thinking about the "stereotypical family where the guy works and the woman doesn't." He clearly values his role as father in a way he had not anticipated.

Few men make such arrangements, but more are involved in the day-to-day routines of taking care of the children. Again Liz:

> He gets up with the kids. He gets up at five-thirty and takes a shower so that when they're up at six, he's ready to go. I get up at six, go to the Y, and work out for a half an hour. And then I come home, and in the meantime he gives them their breakfast, and then I actually come downstairs at about ten after seven. And I eat my breakfast, and then he gets up and gets dressed.

After this routine, the mom gets the kids dressed and takes them to day care. The parents also take turns staying home from work when a child is sick.

Not all husbands are this cooperative. Phyllis calculates that "I spend the bulk of the time with the baby," because "my husband's bad with fussing, he hands him over." She estimates that "the longest he's spent is maybe five hours with him, and when I got home he was like—" She extends her arms, as if handing over a baby. Phyllis's husband will not bathe the baby because he "could drop him." He demands that there always be food in the house but he will not shop for it, and he never washes a dish. He will some-times watch the baby while she finishes her work. She talked about her schedule the day before the interview and the lack of time to complete her work. She said, "The baby was sick, and my husband was tired, and I was like 'I don't care. You have to watch him. I need three hours today to finish this.'"

Some part-timers try to reduce the conflict between domestic work and the rest of their lives by working at home. Not only does this arrangement eliminate an often lengthy commute and produce more discretionary time for other activities, but it also allows them to shift back and forth among paid work, child care, and domestic labor. Most agree with Amelia, a salaried technical writer who works mostly at home, that working at home eliminates some of the stress of arranging baby-sitters and child care and making sure that domestic chores such as grocery shopping get done. But as she puts it, "It solved some problems, created others." Being at home makes it far too easy for other people to assume that they are doing nothing than can't be interrupted (a subject we will return to).

Finally, many part-timers are able to draw on neighbors and rela-tives, particularly for child care, when they are at work. Despite the generally expressed dislike for institutional day care programs, a few do use them part-time, but a larger number do not. Like Tina, they rely on in-home family day care or on relatives and friends to watch their children: "We tried a day care center for about three months and then after that I chose a woman who did day care in her home. I preferred that better." Relatives are the first preference, but in their absence, the kind of day care run by the "lady down the street" is the next best choice: "A friend of mine had her child with this lady near to her house, and she really liked her, so I went to visit. The three kids she was looking after looked really happy, and she was doing a lot of good stuff with them. We were lucky she had a vacancy straightaway. She's really good."

This preference for family day care is widespread. A few mothers also have relatives in the area on whom they can draw. Ellen, whose baby-sitter is available only two days a week, drops her child off at her mother's on the third day she works. As mobile professionals, however, most do not live near their immediate families, so they tend to rely on neighbors and in-home day care providers for the kinds of help they need.

Virtually every part-timer uses some or all of these kinds of resources to help deal with mundane aspects of their domestic lives. These resources are very much part of their ability to maximize the time they spend on activities they truly value. Not all, however, are entirely successful. As many part-timers told us, everything is fine until there is a crisis. Barbara admits: "It's fine unless she's sick. Sometimes he will stay with her, but most often it's me, unless my mom can come over, but she is not always available. If I'm traveling, it's not so bad because I can leave her with my friend, but you can't leave a sick toddler with someone who has one of her own." Although working part-time allows these parents the opportunity not to leave their children in day care for long hours every day, unless the hours are flexible or the part-timer works at home, a temporary crisis either at work or at home can be disruptive; in that case the need is for backups.

One of the priorities for all the part-timers—and it must be an even bigger priority for parents who work full-time—is a network of support. Who can bring the kids home from soccer if a meeting drags on? Can someone take care of the baby if she or the baby-sitter is sick and there is an important meeting? Sometimes the husband does the job, sometimes an available grandparent, many times a friend or neighbor, but without this network of support in place, mixing work and family, even for part-timers, can be precarious. Nonetheless, the burden on part-timers to keep the family system working is considerably less than it would be if they were working full-time.

But It's Not Perfect

While most of those we interviewed talk about domestic labor as something they have under control, we also heard a great deal about two particular problems they encounter. First was the difficulty of being taken seriously as workers: friends, neighbors, and spouses assume that because you work part-time, you are always available. The problem is particularly acute for homeworkers, but not exclusively for them. Second, and more important, we heard a great deal about the unequal division of labor in the home. Although these factors do not prevent most of our respondents from enjoying both work and their domestic lives, they are indeed problems at times.

"Mommy Works inside the Fence"

For some part-timers, particularly those who work at home, the difficulty of being taken seriously as workers is a matter of finding ways to manage the relationship between work and nonwork time. For others, it is a matter of getting other adults to recognize that they are actually working.

One problem is common to all homeworkers: how to let the children know when one is available and when not. Laura, a contractor–technical writer, has developed a particularly symbolic mechanism for demarcating space and time:

> When you're at work, you're at work; when you're at home, you're at home. If I'm inside the fence I'm at work, if I'm outside the fence I'm—I have a portable play yard, if you've ever seen those—a big fence that you're supposed to connect for an outside playpen. They would never stay in it, so we disconnected the ends and put it around my computer desk and all my work, and mommy works inside the fence. They have the rest of the house.

Another engineer also adopts this strategy of demarcating work time from home time:

> I have a conference call every Thursday at noon for two hours. And I've done a lot of those from home. They'll have a half day at school and they get out at twelve, so they're home at twelve-fifteen. So I just tell them in the morning, "When you come home, I'll be in this call, your sandwiches will be there. You have to be quiet until two." I've got good kids. They know that if— That's the problem with some parents. They promise their kids stuff and they don't deliver. Well, my kids know I'll be off at two. And then I will pay attention to them. They can do their own thing till two.

As other studies of homework have found, styles vary (Nippert-Eng 1996). For everyone who seeks a clear demarcation of time or space, someone else enjoys the capacity to blur boundaries.

> My son was going to day care a half-day. And then we would spend an hour to go to the playground or go shopping or do something together. And then he'd take a nap, and I'd do some more work in the afternoon. Well, I didn't want to get so busy that I would have to put him in day care full-time. I liked having a little break in the middle of the day and spending the extra time. One of the reasons for setting up the business in the first place was to have the flexibility to spend more time with my kids.

Arlene has created a work schedule for herself according to her son's schedule. She works when he naps and goes to day care or, later, school. She also reports that she arranges grocery shopping trips or doctor's appointments during the day. Her workday is not rigid. She runs errands, attends her kids' school events, and takes care of the house during a regular workday.

All the part-timers, not just those who work at home, sometimes find that friends and family "forget" that although they are at home when full-time workers are not, they nonetheless have jobs that prevent them from being available on demand. Linda, an engineer, says: "Because I'm available to volunteer at the school sometimes—and I really enjoy that—some of the moms think I have as much time as they do, and I don't. It's hard sometimes." Laura, the technical writer, makes a very similar point:

> People will say: "Oh, well, you can come and do this any time." Like with the preschool: "Well, you can come to the meeting for this party during preschool." But that's when I work! So people who stay at home don't understand that you're working. Or your neighbors come over all the time and want you to run errands, and your husband will say, "Can't you do this or that today?" I'm like "I've got work I need to do today."

Others find they have to train their friends not to call when they are working or point out to relatives that they are not always available to pick them up from the airport or look after them on visits.

A Second Shift?

Some of the women we talked with are able to share at least some domestic chores with their husbands. Given prevailing gender relations and the fact that our respondents work part-time while their spouses do not, the split is typically not 50/50. Ellen, a part-time salaried engineer for a telecommunications company, describes her household's cooking arrangements this way: "It's usually half and half. My husband cooks, so we kind of take turns with that. He doesn't plan any meals, so if anything is planned, it's up to me. But he will cook, if I tell him what to cook. But if I tell him there's nothing to cook, he'll scrounge around and find something." Ellen has a generous definition of "half and half"; her household, like most of those we heard about, is not egalitarian, but it is not a traditional household in which all the domestic labor is done by the mother, either.

While we encountered some household arrangements like Ellen's, they are a distinct minority. Most of our respondents told us that domestic chores are the primary responsibility of one parent, generally the mother. In some cases, this traditional, unequal domestic division of labor has been there all along, so that shifting to part-time work has had little or no effect. Meredith, for example, describes her husband's role this way: "He helps when he's home, I have to give him credit. He does laundry; not right, but he does it. He'll clean the kitchen. I cook, he cleans, on the nights that he's home. He's a real good dad. He plays with the kids, and he cleans up around the house. But really, it's my domain. It's my responsibility." She argues that this has always been the case; that she has always had to do the bulk of the domestic labor. There have been some changes recently, but largely because of her husband's new career as a franchise owner, not because she has gone to work part-time. These changes have not fundamentally altered the domestic division of labor; her husband is home more in the mornings, so he helps out more then. But because he is away more in the evening and has to travel a great deal, Meredith does not feel that the division of labor has been significantly altered.

Even more common is the situation in which part-time work has resulted in a change in our respondents' domestic arrangements. While both partners were working full-time, many couples had developed more egalitarian relationships, sharing cooking and cleaning chores. Diane and Melissa are typical:

> Diane: His mom stayed home and did all the cooking and cleaning and I think he kind of expected me to do that, but I made it clear from the beginning that we did this together.
> Melissa: We would alternate dinner and the rest of the chores. Or we would eat out a lot.

These women, after all, are committed professionals. The women in engineering and computing especially have often struggled hard against stereotypes at work. At an early stage in their education, they made a choice to pursue a career that was nontraditional for women. They are not the kind to accept easily a traditional division of labor at home, and many describe their marriages before they had children as highly egalitarian.

After the women reduce their workday, however, the situation usually changes. Even though the reason for working part-time is often the arrival of children—a time when there is more household work to do—husbands often expect their wives to pick up more of the household chores, most notably the preparation of a family dinner. Other women find themselves expected to take over the largest share of housework and come close to working a second shift. Nancy, an engineer, describes the change:

> That was part of our agreement, that who stayed home would do the chores to free the other person, who isn't home nearly as much, to have those times for the child. Cooking, we used to share cooking because we got home at the same time. We go out to eat less because I'm here now to make it. House cleaning, the grocery shopping—all the grocery shopping—pretty much the coordination of keeping the house maintained is mine now.

Laura, a Ph.D. computational chemist who has been doing beta testing and documentation on a part-time contract basis, echoes this observation:

> I'm definitely doing a higher percentage than I used to. I hate to cook. I've learned to make a lot of things with less than four ingredients. My husband, unfortunately, has gotten used to walking in the door

and having dinner on the table. When we were both working, we would get home, and we always had the argument that I just wanted whatever I could cook in five minutes and he would want to spend an hour cooking a big, huge meal. Back then, I would be like "Fine, you cook it, and I'll eat it." That very rarely happens anymore.

Nor is it simply a matter of cooking and cleaning. Most of the women we spoke with report that it is they, not their husbands, who are primarily responsible for dealing with domestic crises. While we heard much talk of husbands who were "good," who "played with the kids," who "helped out," it generally is the mother who has to respond if a child becomes ill, if there is a snow day, if the plumber must be called. Working part-time is, in part, an attempt to find a solution to this problem. But it tends to become a slippery slope—since they are home more, have more flexible hours, the women who work part-time find that they are even more likely to be identified as the ones who can respond to the unexpected. As Linda, a part-time environmental engineer, puts it: "All those things that become crises, I take care of because I have the day off."

Given their lack of interest in homemaking, why do part-time technical professionals tolerate these inequalities? Many of them have developed rationalizations to explain why these arrangements are at least tolerable. Some argue that an unequal domestic division of labor is reasonable or play down the degree of inequality. Others have been able to accept the lion's share of domestic labor by transforming it, both in their own minds and to an extent in reality, into something more meaningful.

One of the most common explanations we heard involved defining inequality at home as equitable—"I have more time," "He makes more money," "He works hard," "He has to travel." A few have strongly traditional attitudes about who should do the housework. Angela, a salaried computer scientist working for a company that produces data analysis systems, describes her household division of labor as very unequal and seems unperturbed by it: "I like doing that, I like doing that. I grew up in a very strict ethnic household. And my dad kind of ingrained that in me, so it's been brainwashed into me. You sweep, you move the couch, sweep and move the couch again." She laughs.

Most women, however, had different expectations (and often different arrangements); they have come to a kind of grudging acceptance of domestic inequality on more pragmatic grounds. Sheree, a part-time engineer, says:

I guess I always made it clear that I don't like housework. But you know the fact that I'm home earlier than my husband, in that respect . . . it does make a difference. If I'm home all day, then I end up doing more. On the days that I'm home, I do cook dinner. But he still cleans up the kitchen every night. And . . . If I weren't part-time we'd probably share the laundry but now I do it all.

Others have developed economic justifications for their domestic roles. In talking about how the sharing of domestic labor had diminished after she had children and stopped working full-time, Liz, an engineer, says: "When I was home all the time, I wasn't bringing any income in, it seemed like I should just do the household stuff, following more traditional roles at that point." Liz makes explicit the connection between income and feeling entitled to demand a greater contribution from her husband. When her maternity leave ended, her reduced income "justified" her continuing to do more of the domestic labor than she had done before.

Susan, an engineer employed by a major automobile manufacturer, justifies her (unequal) domestic arrangements by pointing to another familiar reason: "I consider my husband's career to be much more important because he's got much more upward potential than I do." Susan is one of the more strongly career-oriented women with whom we spoke. She continues to hope to move up in her company and is one of the few who aspire to a management position. Effectively, however, she has put this hope on the back burner; she wants to have time for her family and she feels that it is economically rational to take over more of the work at home.

While most of the women we interviewed provide this kind of grudging support for arrangements that leave them with most of the chores, at least a few are less accepting. It is clear that these women are engaged in an ongoing struggle over who will do routine domestic work, although it is also clear that the kinds of arguments we

have been discussing give husbands tools with which they can resist. Beth, married to a real estate assessor, is struggling with her
husband's approach to household work:

> He doesn't do laundry. When I was out of town once, he did the laun-
> dry, and everyone's underwear turned pink. The kids were very upset,
> and he said, "Well, if you're going to criticize how I'm doing it, I'm
> not going to do it," or something like that. We have a kind of differ-
> ent— I don't know if it's personality or just an outlook on things. He
> likes to relax first and work later, and I'd rather get all of the work
> done and then relax. What happens is that the work never gets done,
> so I don't take enough time to relax. I'm working on changing that.

Phyllis describes her husband's resistance: "Yeah. I tried con-
fronting him and he's like, 'Oh, well, you have to ask me.' And I
guess . . . Since we've been married, if I ask him, he'll do it, but he
won't do it on his own. And then we get into the thing. Oh, I'd be a
nag if I said, 'Do this, do that, do this, do that.' " She laughs. She
says she sees a confrontation coming with her husband, because
"I'm starting to feel the pressure."

Other women make use of another strategy, comparing their husbands with other men they know rather than with an ideal standard.
Arlie Russell Hochschild (1989) has noted that many women use
this kind of argument to try to demonstrate that their husbands are
actually "good." Teresa, an automotive engineer, uses precisely
those words in describing her engineer-husband's willingness to
share domestic work: "He's really good. He's really supportive. I'm
fortunate." Yet in the next breath she estimates that she does 90
percent of the domestic labor.

Sarah, too, describes her husband as "good" and winds up admit-
ting that she has been taking on more tasks lately:

> A lot of times he would go back to the store and would buy whatever
> we needed. Or I'd give him a partial list and he'd pick up a few extra
> things. A lot of times he would actually run back while I was putting
> the kids to bed, so he's actually a good house helper—he'll do laundry,
> he'll help clean if we need to clean, he'll run back to the grocery store
> and get stuff. Sometimes, now, I may try to leave the office by three.
> My new favorite thing is to run in the grocery store on my way home,

and have it done before four-thirty or five, when I get back home and pick up Stephanie. So that's my new preference, if I can do it that way. But he's not opposed to pitching in. He's always been good at that.

Some of the women deal with domestic chores by redefining them as child care. Domestic chores are not fulfilling, rewarding work, but if one does them with children, they become "family time," fun, even developmental activities. One technical professional says, "I take the baby with me when I go to the store, and he likes to be with me when I vacuum. I guess that's part of the fun of being home more. We get to do stuff together."

Ellen, a part-time engineer, also emphasizes the social aspect of doing chores:

We do laundry. Emily likes to do laundry. Everything takes longer when you have a two-year-old helping you, so throwing the wash in the washing machine can take up to a half an hour. Just, you know, doing things around the house. I try to get her involved in helping around the house. It takes longer, but at least we're doing it together.

Laura, the technical writer/beta tester, describes her merging of domestic tasks with child care as a combination of expediency and education:

They love to vacuum. They fight over who gets to vacuum. The little one was scared of it for a while, but I worked real hard and let him push it when it wasn't on, and now he loves it. So he gets the big vacuum, and the little one gets the Dirt Devil, and they do a great job. So as long as I'm at home staying with them, they're going to learn that you have to clean, you have to cook, you have to grocery shop.

All of these women do the bulk of the domestic labor in their households. None of them indicates any enthusiasm for doing domestic chores. Their efforts to fuse enjoyable activities with mundane household labor represent a partially successful effort to marginalize chores and to expand the time they spend doing things they find rewarding and worthwhile.

These responses will sound familiar to students of dual-career couples. Many of our respondents slip into conventional roles partly because it is easier to do so, partly because they find it "makes sense." Moreover, these conclusions have been developed in a society in which men are more likely to be defined as breadwinners (Potucheck 1997) and in which traditional assumptions about who should do which labor remain powerful. Even the most optimistic surveys of household labor (Barnett and Rivers 1996, Coltrane 1996) cannot escape the reality that women still do most of the domestic labor in most households. In this sense, there is real reason to be concerned that part-time work can become a "reason" for women to continue to do most of the domestic work.

At the same time, to reduce this concern to the argument that part-time work is simply a "mommy trap" is to ignore the fact that most of our respondents have successfully limited the amount of time and effort they devote to routine domestic chores. It is very unusual for the women we interviewed to say that domestic labor interferes significantly with their ability to do the things they really want to do. The tendency to revert to traditional patterns at home is certainly a potential threat to the kinds of lives they want to lead, but most of the part-time professionals we encountered do not experience that threat as immediate. For them it appears to be a kind of residual problem, one they are able to manage. Since it doesn't prevent them from enjoying both work and domestic life, they can accept it.

Reconfiguring the Package

No matter how committed one is to the workplace, household work doesn't go away because there is no longer a family member devoting her (or, for that matter, his) full time to it. Someone needs to do the chores and take care of the children. In many parts of Europe the state has taken over much of the responsibility for child care, offering subsidized child care programs and programs for before and after school. It also provides extended paid leave for parents. In the United States, this option has proved to be politically difficult, and household work remains the sole responsibility of the family, even when both parents work.

Those to whom we spoke cope with this responsibility in ways that enable them to feel satisfied about both their work and their domestic lives. Their solution is not shared parenting; rather, it is a refusal to embrace a traditional domestic role. The women are far from committed to being traditional housewives, nor do they agree that it is women's role to take care of the home and protect it from the influence of the outside world. What our respondents try to do at home, as they have done at work, is to reconfigure the traditional package.

One key to their success in doing so is their willingness and ability to commodify some of these tasks. McDonald's may not have been quite what the feminist pioneers imagined when they wrote about collective dining facilities, but any visit to a suburban fast-food restaurant during midweek daytime hours provides evidence of the role they play in family life. Although the people with whom we talked resist putting their children in large-scale institutional day care for long hours every day, they are willing to use family day care for shorter lengths of time, as long as it does not deprive them of time to be with their children. Many use cleaners, baby-sitters, and other paid services to help at home. For conservative supporters of the mommy-track version of part-time, our respondents are disappointments. They are not afraid of using fast food and a cleaning team if that will help.

To avoid full-scale commodification of family life, men and women also share some of the chores, while friends, family, and negotiated parental sharing take care of the rest of the child care needs. And most important, they consciously limit the effort and time they devote to domestic work. Domestic labor is something to be "got out of the way"; it is not for them, as it is for the traditional housewife, an all-consuming task involving commitment of enormous energy and resources.

Most Americans continue to lack the financial resources to hire outside help and the opportunity to negotiate customized work hours. Moreover, not all women can withstand the pressures to take over all the domestic labor, especially if it becomes routine to be at home more than their husbands are. The successful institutionalization of these new arrangements may depend on men's adoption of customized hours too. Indeed, our respondents' experiences suggest that it is this solution, far more than shared parenting, that will lead to a real reorganization of family life. Shared parenting, while certainly desirable and helpful, is not in itself the means by which men and women are likely to put work (either paid or domestic) in its place. Equal sharing of traditional work and domestic roles simply involves a division of unsatisfying responsibilities. Neither party is likely to be satisfied with such an arrangement. What our respondents have been able to do is to redefine both work and domestic roles. They have reorganized both aspects of their lives so that they are able to focus on those aspects of them they find most rewarding.

7

"When Are You Coming Back to Work Full-Time?"

The people we met have worked hard to put together a new identity that integrates work into a broader framework and to put together a package of resources that allows them to pursue the rest of their dreams without sacrificing their commitment to work. While they have incurred some costs in creating this package, they have been surprisingly successful. The question remains, however: How long can it last? Epstein and her colleagues (1999) call the part-time lawyers they met "time deviants" because they spend fewer hours at work each week than their colleagues. The term suggests the problem: part-timers are subjected to social pressure to "normalize" their lives.

Indeed, voluntary part-time work is usually thought of as a short-term option. The most common image is of someone (usually a woman) who, because of a need linked to a particular period in the life course (such as the need to care for a child or a sick relative), has opted to reduce her work hours for a few months or a few years. When the child reaches school age or the relative recovers or dies, the part-time professional returns to the full-time workforce. Part-time work, in other words, is typically defined as abnormal, as an interruption, as a temporary departure from the normal rhythm of professional work time.

The limited research that has been done on part-time professionals supports this stereotype and suggests that people tend to work part-time for finite, often relatively brief periods. Analysis of National Opinion Research Center data by Phyllis Moen (1985) showed that while a majority of women had worked part-time at some point between 1972 and 1976, persistent part-time work was unusual. Rebecca Blank's (1989) analysis of the Panel Study of Income Dynamics similarly shows that part-time work tends to be a short-term expedient. More recently, Mindy Fried's (1998) case study of an insurance company found that most employees, including professionals, who took advantage of the option to reduce their work hours did so for a limited time. Indeed, the few who had worked part-time for an extended period were regarded unfavorably by other part-timers. Anita Garey (1999) describes much part-time work for women as "sequencing"—a phase through which women go as they attempt to integrate work and motherhood.

Even advocates of expanded opportunities for part-time work tend to view part-time work as temporary, an interruption of one's "normal" career. A vast literature on family-friendly work policies is almost unanimous on this point. Such policies invariably are promoted as allowing workers to deal with events or crises associated with specific periods in the life course. The assumption is always that workers will return to full-time status when the event is over or the crisis has passed. Even Lotte Bailyn (1993), whose *Breaking the Mold* articulated a more systematic critique of the structure of work time in professional and managerial careers, sees part-time work as a phase, something one does temporarily when one is stepping off the fast track for a time.

Despite the apparent consensus that part-time work is a short-term interruption in one's work life, our respondents' experiences point to a more complex reality. We certainly heard a great deal about pressures, both formal and informal, to return to full-time employment, but we also encountered people who have been able to sustain part-time schedules for surprisingly long periods. Some of these people were contractors, for whom time limits on part-time work boil down to their own ability to tolerate the financial sacrifice. But some of them are organizational employees who have found ways to stretch out their stints as part-timers for longer than is generally thought possible. The existence of both groups suggests that the prevailing structures of time are more flexible than is generally acknowledged.

The question "How long can it last?" implies another: What do part-timers actually want? If people simply want to "step out" for a short time, pressures to return to a full-time schedule represent a relatively minor inconvenience. If, however, they wish to work reduced hours for longer periods, then such pressures are far more problematic. The prevailing assumption is that part-time work is a phase that will soon end. Framing part-time work as part of family-friendly policies reveals this assumption, since it roots part-time work in the need to deal with specific, temporally bounded life events.

In listening to our respondents talk about what they envisaged in the future, we found, again, that reality is more complex than is generally acknowledged. We did encounter part-timers who define part-time work as a short-term expedient and who plan to return to full-time work after a brief interval. We also met people who want to continue working reduced hours indefinitely. Some of these are contractors and employees who have succeeded in creating longer-term part-time options for themselves. Others talk about long-term part-time work in terms that are more theoretical: they think about it, even desire it, but believe that prevailing realities make such arrangements improbable.

Some part-timers, then, perhaps many, are resisting the "ideal worker" norm described by Joan Williams (2000). If they can, they will choose reduced work schedules for prolonged periods. But will they have the opportunity?

How Employers Define Short-Term Work as Abnormal

We have seen that employers work hard to keep part-time work an exception to normal practice. A strict time limit on how long employees can work part-time is often an important part of this strategy. In effect, they define it as a kind of leave, granted for a finite period for a carefully defined reason (maternity, family illness, education). This is the model offered by the company that employs Holly as an engineer:

They just announced a policy over the phone. What word did they
use? "Assurance." An employee that requests part-time or flextime
for elder care or child care is assured, unless there's a really grave exception for some reason, for business reasons, it is assured that they
can have that for a period of three years. I have a problem with the
three years. Once they start getting school age, that's when you're
needed more than ever. The basic moral learning and that's when the
real parenting skills kick in. So I have a problem with three years. I
don't know. I'm being strongly encouraged right now to increase
hours.

She is not entirely happy.

A number of employers do have explicit policies stipulating the
maximum length of time an employee can work part-time. Typically, these periods are relatively short. Three years is at the long
end of the spectrum; most policies are considerably more restrictive. Many employers do not have such formal policies, but they
can create very explicit mechanisms that serve the same function. It
is common, for example, to encounter employees who have negotiated individual part-time contracts that specify when they will return to full-time status. At least one engineer we met has to renego-
tiate her part-time status every year. While this practice does not
preclude a renewal, it places the burden on her regularly to justify
her continuation as a part-time employee.

Even when there are no explicit requirements about return dates,
other factors pressure part-timers to return to work full-time sooner
rather than later. An obvious factor is the economic penalty imposed on part-time employees. While some employers do offer prorated benefits to part-time employees, most of our respondents lost
some or all of their benefits by reducing their work hours. Although
most can depend on their spouse's benefit package, the employer
has clearly created an economic incentive to resume full-time work.

Equally significant is the effect of reducing work hours on salaries
and promotion opportunities. Some of our respondents indicate that
part-time employees may not receive consideration for a salary increase; as one engineer put it, "raises stop" when you work part-
time. As we have seen, it is unusual to promote part-time employees, and we encountered some who were required to accept a
demotion in exchange for reduced hours. Whatever technical profes-

sionals' ambivalence about promotions, many would undoubtedly benefit economically by returning to full-time work.

Even employee evaluations can serve as a form of pressure to expand work hours. Barbara, a computer scientist, explained that her managers did not change their approach to evaluating her after she reduced her hours; they evaluated her as if she worked full-time. In her words, "I think they forget; but I don't think they adjust [their evaluations] for you because you're part-time." Even though she claims that her evaluations have actually improved since she has been working part-time, she still experiences the evaluation as pressure to work more.

Some organizations' policies serve as reminders to part-timers that they have been, in effect, demoted. Jennifer and Lisa, the jobsharers, complained about their employer's practice of defining their organization as a series of rings and banishing part-timers and contractors to the outer ring. Marna, a chemical engineer, remembered another kind of symbolic demotion: "I noticed that on the organization chart they usually go alphabetically, but once we went part-time, me and this other woman, we were out of alphabetical order and always on the bottom. They put little 'pts' by us, so that you knew. It was kind of a way of making sure that you knew we were there, but we're not equal."

Finally, the head-count policy that plays a role in discouraging part-time status by treating part-timers as functionally equivalent to full-time employees also pressures them to return to full-time status as soon as possible.

As our comments about the discretion of individual managers imply, not all of the incentives to return to full-time status are the result of formal policies. On the contrary, some of the most powerful pressures are informal. Many respondents report being continually asked when they will be returning to full-time status, and are pressured to name a return date. When we asked Nancy, an engineer, how long she planned to go on working part-time, she was only partly joking when she quipped, "My employer would pay a lot of money to know the answer to that question."

Even ostensibly polite, welcoming behavior on the part of managers can exert a subtle pressure to resume full-time status. Barbara, while denying that she has experienced explicit pressure to name a return date (though she reports that other part-time employees have), says, "I've been told that any time I want to go full-time again, that would be great."

Informal pressure to return to a full-time schedule also comes from the volume of work. As many studies of reduced work have shown, part-timers often experience pressure to stretch the limits of their workday, to stay a little later or to take work home. Our respondents are no exception. We heard many stories about taking work home, staying longer than one is technically supposed to, answering calls at home, and the like. Many respondents grumble about this kind of thing but seem to have little ability to resist it. John, an engineer working for an electronics company, confesses, "I am still leaving late after work. I need to get that down. I need to work more like twenty-five hours." The "I need to get that down" has the abstract quality of the promise one makes oneself to break a bad habit.

In some cases, the volume of work leads to more than just the occasional late night or intrusion of work into family time. Barbara describes how her schedule has evolved since she returned from her initial maternity leave and began working part-time:

> And then I came back three days a week. That didn't last too long because then I got a lot of pressure to increase my hours. I was working like twenty-five hours. But I had a lot of pressure to increase my hours, so I went to four days a week, and I stayed there for two and a half years. And then I was home for five months. When I came back with my second, I came back five days. I soon after that went to thirty-two hours.

As she indicates, this gradual escalation in work time is a response, at least in part, to external pressure. She responded to this pressure incrementally, and is now trying to persuade herself, against the evidence, that the pressure has diminished:

> At this point, I don't get too much pressure to work additional. And I don't mind doing a little bit of overtime as long as I can do it in the evenings, maybe after the children go to bed. And there are times when I participate in conference calls from home, and if there's something important going on and if it happens to be when I'm home with the kids, I'll join in on the conference call.

Later, in talking about how her work is evaluated, she confesses that she thinks her company has forgotten that she is working part-time and, in effect, puts the same kind of pressure on her that they put on full-timers.

Interestingly, she believes that this pressure does not stem entirely from her employer's ideological reluctance to allow people to work part-time. She attributes it, in part, to the changing rhythm of technical work and organizational policies.

> I just think of where we are in this project, it's that we need more people. Yeah, we could bring people in, but they're not as good, they're not as useful immediately as the people that are already on the project. They've been on board on the project, so I guess it's a matter of where we are, and there's always much more work than there are people. Always so much work. It does seem to me that it gets worse with time. We used to have a much longer interval to do projects, but now as the competition gets tougher and customers expect more, our intervals have shrunk. And quite a lot, too. We used to do projects in like two and a half years, and now everything scoots up to eighteen months. And that's the nature of the beast, that's the competitive marketplace that we're in.

In short, when the volume and pace of work increase but staffing does not, managers, unsurprisingly, put pressure on part-time workers to work additional hours and to return to full-time status.

The organizational pressures to limit the duration of part-time employment are not limited to the efforts of individual managers. On the contrary, most of our respondents indicate that the pressures they experience are pervasive, coming from colleagues, from the culture of the workplace, and, in a sense, from within. Mindy Fried (1998) refers to a "culture of overtime" that dominates the company she studied. Gideon Kunda (1992) suggests that overtime is a normal part of the culture of technical organizations and serves an important role in motivation and control. Thus even when managers are supportive and do little or nothing to pressure part-timers to increase their hours, they experience pressure to do so anyway. While these cultural pressures—at least outside of start-up companies—are perhaps not as extreme as those experienced by New York lawyers (Epstein et al. 1999), they are nevertheless real. We encountered several technical professionals who regard a 40-hour week as a "reduced" work schedule; many tell about having put in extremely long hours of work at various points in their careers.

The role of colleagues in reinforcing the culture of overtime is not uniform. Indeed, some of our respondents comment on how supportive of their part-time schedules their colleagues have been. Their willingness to arrange meetings at times when part-timers can attend, to pinch-hit for them at times when they cannot be physically present, and so on are cited by several respondents as keys to their ability to function as part-timers. Ellen, an engineer, describes her colleagues as "receptive" to her three-day-a-week schedule. Occasionally someone expects her to attend a meeting on one of her days off or to complete work on a schedule that doesn't work for her, but usually the person is simply unfamiliar with her schedule. She is able to deal with these problems simply by saying no or by emphasizing her availability at home. Ellen even points to her part-time schedule as beneficial to her colleagues in some ways: "Actually, there's a benefit to being here three days a week, because there's always a lag time. So then if I give something to somebody on a Tuesday, they're like, 'Oh, you want it tomorrow.' I say, 'Oh, no, I don't need it till Thursday.' They're like 'Oh!'"

Others, however, experience pressure from colleagues to conform to a "normal" intense schedule. Some, like Holly, complain about various forms of teasing: "I get stuff all the time, not from my management chain, they're extremely liberal-minded and great, but from peers or from people in other departments that I interact with, male and female. I get all sorts of comments, 'You're on the mommy track' or 'You don't care.'"

Some encounter complaints about scheduling problems or questions about when they plan to return to full-time work. A particularly common irritation is quasi-humorous expressions of jealousy. Lucy, an automotive engineer, complains that many of the male engineers with whom she works say, "Oh, I wish I could have done that, ha-ha-ha." She regards these comments as insincere, since she doesn't believe they would accept the reduction in pay. Rather, she perceives them as evidence of disapproval and a reminder of her "special status." The effect is reminiscent of what Rosabeth Moss Kanter (1977) found in her analysis of exaggerated politeness among male managers: when male managers ostentatiously alter their behavior because "there's a lady present," they are reminding the "lady" that she is "the other" and that her presence makes everyone else uncomfortable.

Finally, some appear to have internalized the culture of overtime and wrestle with themselves over the question of how long a workday should be. Many are very proud of their ability to get as much work done on a part-time schedule as they had as full-timers. Indeed, as we argued earlier, this is strong evidence of their unwavering commitment to their work as professionals. Yet this commitment to high professional standards also places psychological limits on part-time work for some of our respondents. Lucy, the automotive engineer, confesses that she frequently works more than her scheduled 24 hours a week. She describes her work unit as understaffed, acknowledging that the work load she confronts is artificially created. Yet she does not resist and argues that the need she feels to keep up with the work load is "probably just my own pressure. I just always feel that I should. My supervisor would be supportive if I didn't. If I worked exactly eight hours [on one of her three workdays], took my lunch, that would be no problem. But there's just so much, and it's accumulating so fast, that I have to do that and more." In effect, she and the other part-time technical professionals who feel similarly do not experience the culture of overtime solely as an external force; at times they impose it on themselves.

In sum, part-time technical professionals find themselves in a work world that defines what they do as abnormal. They are, as Epstein and her colleagues suggest, "time deviants" whose experience is either implicitly or explicitly compared unfavorably to the normal long workday by virtually everyone: managers, colleagues, even themselves. In very few workplaces is part-time work defined as normal or considered to be as valid as the full-time day.

Part-Time All the Time?

Somewhat surprisingly, the behavior of many of our part-time respondents—including those who talk about wanting to "pull their own weight"—suggests they do not fully share the dominant view that part-time work is a short-term expedient. Many, in fact, have already worked reduced hours far longer than the few months or a year or two that they had originally anticipated. Many others are discovering that part-time schedules are very attractive and imagine themselves working in this way a long time, perhaps indefinitely.

True, most of our respondents began part-time work by negotiating a finite part-time stint with a "return" date after one or two years. Phyllis, a computer scientist, is typical. Her part-time job developed as a kind of extension of her maternity leave. After exhausting her twelve-week maternity leave (six weeks with pay, six without) and using up several weeks of accumulated vacation time, she returned to work three days a week. Her employer agreed to this schedule, on the assumption that she would return to work full-time twelve months after her maternity leave had begun. In the meantime, she and her husband are trying out various baby-sitting arrangements in anticipation of her return to full-time status.

The context in which she is making this decision, however, suggests that Phyllis is much more ambivalent about defining part-time work as a short-term expedient than might initially appear. She clearly indicates that her decision is shaped by her perception of organizational realities. In effect, she fears that this is all that is possible and is concerned about the negative consequences of trying for more:

> I was more worried that they would say no, you couldn't do it, and I really, really agonized over that for a long, long time before I approached anyone here. And I did do a little research. There was an environmental engineer . . . after the birth of her second child, she quit completely, but she had gone part-time after the birth of her first child and they were very accommodating. She even worked at home and things like that and her arrangement was for a year. She was going to do it part-time and then come back full-time. Well, at the end of that year she decided she didn't want to come back full-time so there was—and you hear all this through the grapevine—there was a little bit of tension there because she had said she was coming back and that's what they expected and then she said, "Well, wait a minute, no, I don't want to." And it wasn't long after that she became pregnant again, and so I was concerned about that. And then she quit. And environmental engineers, especially women, are like gold. That's why I think they really bent over backward to try to accommodate her. And then the way I look at it, she kind of blew them off, and I felt, God, what's that going to do for me?

She still plans to return to full-time work after a year, but admits that she is still thinking about it, trying out baby-sitting arrangements, willing to reconsider. When asked how long she intends to stay on a part-time schedule, she appears almost to be talking herself into the return date she initially arranged:

> I've been very happy with the sitter that we found. We went through a few changes when we were figuring out exactly how much more or less we were taking in. And I told my husband, you know, I could see myself easily going to four days a week. If I can't decide at the end of that year, I may ask them can I just stay part-time. I guess we'll see how it works, although I have confidence in the woman I take the baby to. If at the end of the year, if they said, "If you don't come back full-time, you don't have a job," I would probably feel comfortable coming back full-time.

This fatalistic acceptance of what appears to be possible combined with a temptation to try for more is characteristic of many of those who have made only short-term arrangements.

Some technical professionals have succeeded in carving out long-term part-time arrangements for themselves. The most obvious way is to become a contractor. Setting up on one's own largely eliminates the kinds of pressures we have been discussing; employers' concerns about head counts, loyalty, and other issues do not apply to the self-employed. Walt, an engineer who has worked as a contractor for more than a decade, exemplifies what is possible. By his account, he has lucked into a part-time contract arrangement with a company that produces metal products, and he expects to be able to maintain this relationship indefinitely.

We also encountered organizational employees who have been working reduced hours longer than is typical. We interviewed five who have worked part-time for five years or more, one as long as ten years. We encountered numerous people who have been working part-time for two to five years. Most of them have done so by actively resisting, often at some personal cost, employers' pressures to return full-time. Many part-timers also clearly hope to continue working part-time for considerable lengths of time, even beyond the years when they have preschoolers at home.

When they have the option to negotiate open-ended part-time arrangements, they take advantage of them. Tina, an engineer who has been working part-time for six and a half years (five of them in a job-share), claims, "I've never considered coming back full-time." She explains:

> I have three kids, I have a seven-year-old in first grade, and then I have twin two-year-olds. I wouldn't even think about it until they're in school all day. And I bet even then, it's just so much easier to . . . Like today, I went to the grocery store and I'm doing three loads of laundry. And on Monday I did another three loads of laundry. And I get all my errands run, and on the weekends you can actually enjoy yourself and your kids. It's much easier for my family than if I were full-time. And if I were full-time, it would be fifty or sixty hours a week, not forty. So I don't even consider it.

Even in the face of real pressures to return to full-time status, some technical professionals clearly intend to work part-time for an extended period. Nancy, the female engineer who referred to her company's open desire to know when she plans to go back to full-time status, describes her plans this way:

> Until my son is school age, I will definitely stay home. I would not put him in day care. We have frankly checked out a good school—a Christian school that we were looking at that's on the way to work— and our plan would be that one of us would drop him off and the other would pick him up in the evening. So until he goes to school, the plan is to stay home with him. I do hope to return to the work-force full-time, but never in a way that leaves him a latchkey child. But our current jobs are flexible enough that my husband could go in early and come home early, and I could go in late and I could come home late.

The implications are clear: only if both parents' jobs can be structured in such a way that the child is always cared for by one of them will she consider going back to work full-time.

Part-Time Work and the Rejection of Conventional Work Time

Only a minority of part-time workers are able to sustain their reduced work arrangements longer than a year or two, reflecting, in
part, employers' continued resistance to long-term part-time
arrangements. Contracting provides an alternative way to arrange
part-time schedules, but not everyone is willing or able to become
self-employed. Among both long-term and short-term part-timers,
however, we found many who are uncomfortable with the prevailing time structures of the contemporary workplace. They want flexible work schedules that are more than short-term solutions to specific problems.

The ability to control one's time is a priority for virtually everyone we interviewed. They are very clear that it is not just the number of hours they work that matters. In fact, some are satisfied with
relatively minor reductions in work hours—cutting back to four
days a week, say, or working 30–35 hours (which may actually represent a significant reduction). They echo Robinson and Godbey's
(1997) argument that the problem is feeling rushed, and one can
feel rushed even when one is working a relatively modest number
of hours. As Cynthia Negrey (1993) argues, the desire to work part-
time is really about the desire to manage one's time, to be able to
work in such a way as to be able to do other things comfortably and
conveniently. Ellen Galinsky (1999) has argued that employees
seek to "navigate" the relationship between work and other aspects
of their lives, not simply to balance them. The emphasis our respondents place on controlling one's time, on flexibility, on working out an arrangement that works for them, is clearly what she has
in mind.

Many of the contractors are particularly emphatic about the importance of controlling their time. Some arrange their workdays
around the other things they want or need to do. When asked about
their typical workday, they speak of working early in the morning,
during naps, after the children have gone to bed; they experience
this scattershot approach not as oppressive but as giving them a degree of autonomy. Others want to be able to tailor their work to
their frame of mind on any given day. This is the key reason that

Claire, a technical writer, will not accept a salaried position, "primarily because I don't want to have to go through the motions of going to work every day, regardless of whatever I feel like, and dressing up regardless of whatever I feel like and answering to the same person all the time."

Still others use contracting as a way of varying their work effort across the calendar year; for them, managing one's time implies the ability to take time off to do something else. Ben, an electrical engineer, said:

> I think it would be great if I could make a living on just six months a year. I think that this country has gone way overboard on time commitment to work. The Europeans are in the right direction in terms of everybody starts with six weeks off. That life is too short, too personal, to spend it all for somebody else. A lot of people go in and make their job very personal; their livelihood becomes them, but it's not . . . I'm more of an individualist.

Ben talks approvingly of his retired father's ability to enjoy life, and he hopes he won't have to wait until he retires to enjoy his own life. He has been involved in community theater in several states, and he wants to be able to take time off for that and for outdoor sports. Despite the variety of meanings attached to "managing one's time," all of these contractors share a dislike for the regimented, inflexible quality of time in full-time organizational employment.

Our corporate respondents also negotiated a wide variety of schedules, reflecting the different needs they are trying to accommodate. Some want one day off a week to do errands so that they can enjoy their weekends. Others want to leave work early to pick up their kids from school. Some have negotiated homework arrangements to enable them to be with their kids while they work. All part-time employees, in effect, have customized their work time. Nevertheless, they still have complaints. Barbara admits that she is contemplating returning to full-time work. When we ask why, she complains that working part-time intensifies the way she works—she feels as if she is squeezing a full-time job into a part-time schedule. "I'm so wound up and it's just hard for me to switch, to go from work to home playing with the kids." June, another computer scientist, grumbles that a policy change at work has forced her to move from hourly to salaried status. The problem is not simply that her hours have increased to 35 a week (still considered part-time by her employer). Rather, it is that she has lost some control over her hours, even though she acknowledges that her employer monitored her time more closely when she was being paid by the hour:

> The only problem now is that I can't be flexible. Before, if I was on a project and I worked more than the twenty-four hours, I would just write it in on my time sheet. Now, if I work more than thirty-five, I'm not going to get paid for more than thirty-five. Or if I suddenly say that this isn't working out, I want to work thirty hours . . . It's a lot more hassle to adjust up or down.

Part-timers such as the engineer-dancer and the contractor whose alcohol problems made full-time work impractical clearly want long-term part-time arrangements. But what about the majority of the technical professionals with whom we spoke, for whom part-time work is a response to having children? Here, one could argue, is a group of people who have no need for longer-term arrangements.

While it is true that some of the parent part-timers we met see their arrangements as temporary, while their children are small, many others see the need for flexibility as extending well beyond the first few years of their children's lives. Many have several children, so that even someone who intends to return to work when her children are in school needs to work part-time for more than five years, perhaps considerably more. Moreover, we met parents who found, often to their surprise, that their desire for flexible hours did not end when their children were in school. Maria, a software engineer who has been working part-time or job-sharing for more than six years, has two children, aged six and two and a half; she seems unsure that she will return to full-time status when her youngest enters school:

> I don't have any plans to change it at this point, I really don't. I've made the comment, as long as it's ideal, at this point, I don't want the full-time. I may change my mind when they're in school all day; I

have to believe I can still occupy myself for two days a week! You know, I really enjoy it, being able to do what I want to do and not all the time.

Like other technical professionals among our respondents, Maria really enjoys the experience of working part-time and does not experience it as a hardship or sacrifice. She also finds that her attitude toward part-time work is evolving; she is considering extending her reduced work arrangements longer than she had intended. Again, not everyone we met shares this experience; but many do find themselves unwilling to give up flexibility.

In addition to emphasizing flexibility, part-timers express considerable antipathy to the culture of overtime in professional work. Their attitudes are complex and at times even contradictory, since, as we have seen, many have internalized the prevailing belief that long hours at work are normal. Yet at the same time they object to the implicit assumption that work is the most important thing in their lives, even the only thing that matters. These people, as we have seen, have made remarkable efforts to preserve work as a significant part of their lives; what they object to is the impossibility of having what they define as a meaningful life when work time is both inflexible and extremely long.

Philip, an electrical engineer working for a small producer of hand-held computers, expresses this critique quite clearly. He has deliberately chosen to work for this small company because it offers him the assurance of what he sees as a "reduced" workweek—40 hours. He praises his boss's approach, which he attributes to negative experiences the boss had at another company:

> I think that's really just what he thinks works out best because, with his experience over at his previous company—I think a lot of it came from his negative experiences over there with it. Because they would have cases where there would be a meeting about a product that was just about ready, and the marketing people would say, "Well, what about this, this, this, and this? You'll have that ready for us on Friday, right?" And there was no ifs, ands, or buts about it. They had to have something, so they would work three days straight—they wouldn't go home. My boss didn't like that, so he decided to go back to the forty-hour week—if it can't be done that week, it can wait.

Philip explained why he, too, rejects these "unreasonable" time demands:

> I really believe in the necessity of the integrity of a good family. And working twelve- to fourteen-hour days—sixty-to eighty-hour weeks— is not conducive to a good family. I've seen other families where they have had a lot of problems because of that. I missed a little bit because at one time my dad was working a job where he would get home later in the evening, and I missed having him at home. So I decided, if possible, to avoid those kinds of jobs.

Barbara, the software engineer, told a story early in our interview that she initially framed as a story about dedication (although there is also an element of incredulity in her account):

> It's a very demanding environment here. People are very dedicated and they normally put in a lot of hours, and so when you work part-time, you're not one of them. People here can be incredible, the hours, and the sacrifices they make for the company. I just, a little while ago, this is just an example, we had a meeting and this one woman was supposed to be at this meeting and her son, her toddler-age son, was taken to the emergency room, and she said she would call in to the meeting from the hospital. And it was serious; it was a congenital heart problem. People are very dedicated here.

Later she returned to this story, this time making it clear that she refuses to embrace this kind of behavior as acceptable or normal: "I'll always be an ambitious person, but I guess there is a limit to the sacrifices I'll make. I won't call in to a meeting from a hospital emergency room. That's not a sacrifice I'll make."

We heard numerous stories like this, reflecting a sense that the demands of work are unreasonable, that it is not worth it to succumb to them, that it is not possible to have an enjoyable life while working under these conditions. Some share Angela's inability to understand people who have work stations at home so they can continue working after hours; she describes such people as "junkies" and confesses that she'd "rather go the zoo." Having a life, for this group of technical professionals, includes work—they are not reject-ing it at all. But life extends beyond work to a range of other activi-ties that they define as worthwhile and gratifying.

Customizing Work

The prevailing view of part-time workers is of a relatively homo-geneous group of people with a short-term need for a reduced work schedule. The part-time technical professionals with whom we spoke pointed to a different reality. In spite of the considerable pres-sures to return to full-time work, some of them have worked part-time for five or more years either as contractors or as salaried em-ployees. Still more aspire to such arrangements, or at least are greatly critical of the inflexibility of organizational time and what they perceive as the unreasonable time pressures imposed on profes-sional employees. What many seek is a choice that allows them to fit their work schedules into an evolving set of desires. They want an institutional flexibility that matches the flexibility they see in their nonwork lives.

Not all part-timers want to work part-time indefinitely, but some do. Their approaches here, as in other aspects of part-time work, vary considerably. Some accept the prevailing definition of part-time work as a short-term expedient and plan to return to full-time work. Others also plan to return to full-time status eventually, but either are toying with the idea of extending their part-time arrangements or have actu-ally done so. Still others appear not to intend to return to full-time status. Some of the contractors we met are happy (and able) to con-tinue their arrangements indefinitely. But the talk we heard from or-ganizational professionals about "ideal arrangements," about enjoy-ing their situation, about being reluctant to go back to their old work schedules also suggests an openness to a different way of working.

We are not suggesting that all or even most part-time technical professionals are consciously rebelling against the corporate ap-proach to time. We do believe, however, that in various ways these technical professionals are exploring an alternative approach to the problem of work time. We are struck by the fact that the various ap-proaches to part-time work are not distinct alternatives; rather, they bleed into one another, as individuals who start out approaching part-time work in one way begin to explore or discover other ways of approaching it. The evolving character of their approach to part-time work and the unwillingness of many of them to settle for a short-term version of it expose the limitations inherent in defining the time problem as a phase, an interruption in the normal work schedule. As Lotte Bailyn (1993) has noted, this attitude promotes a "solution at the margins," a systematic making of exceptions for individuals who have these short-term needs. It leaves intact Williams's (2000) "ideal worker norm"—the assumption that the typical worker can and should give more or less undivided attention to paid work. It is precisely this expectation that our respondents' experiences call into question.

Rather than a solution at the margins, the technical professionals we met want the ability to customize work time. To customize one's time is to go beyond one-size-fits-all family-friendly policies that frame part-time work as a short-term tactic structured along lines set by the employer; it is to exercise true control over one's work time, to choose freely among a range of options, including short-term, extended, and even permanent reduced work arrangements. The professionals with whom we spoke were unusual in their ability to come so close to this degree of customization. Their experiences suggest both what is wrong with contemporary family-friendly policies and what might be possible for other groups of workers.

8

Customizing Time:
Obstacles and Strategies

"What is this life if, full of care, / We have no time to stand and stare." The lines come from W. H. Davies's poem "Leisure," and may be the only lines anyone remembers from an otherwise undistinguished poet and writer of Baptist hymns. Davies was writing nearly a hundred years ago but he might also have been speaking for the people we heard from who want time to play with their children, to be with their spouse, to sing, act, or dance, to volunteer in the community, or to travel. Too often the argument for reducing work time is framed in terms of worker productivity and retention, as if these were the only things that mattered. Alternatively it focuses exclusively on the need to make "concessions" to employees' short-term family needs. This may be the best way to persuade employers to cooperate, but much is lost when alternate visions of the good life are excluded from the discussion. What the people we talked with want from life may vary in the details, but the overall picture is remarkably consistent. Both those who sought reduced work schedules for family reasons and those who had other motivations are not satisfied with lives centered on endlessly demanding jobs limited only by momentary breaks when time demands become unmanageable. They want a life that has room for a variety of activities.

We should take care, however, not to fall into the Romantic trap of denigrating work altogether. The people we spoke with envisage lives that include work; indeed, rewarding work so enhances their lives that they have gone to great lengths to preserve it. One could counterpose to Davies's emphasis on leisure the words of another critic of industrialism:

> It may be proved, with much certainty, that God intends no man to live in this world without working: but it seems to me no less evident that He intends every man to be happy in his work. . . . Now in order that people may be happy in their work, these three things are needed: They must be fit for it: They must not do too much of it: and they must have a sense of success in it. (Ruskin 1851)

Perhaps because many of our respondents are women who have fought hard for positions in male-dominated professions, they communicate the joy of work. Perhaps it is because technology is an exciting and fashionable field, as it was in the nineteenth century. Perhaps, too, it is because they have time to appreciate work's pleasures, and spending time away from work reminds them why they enjoy their engineering, programming, designing, and writing. Work is a central interest, a central part of the identity of everyone with whom we spoke. But they can enjoy neither work nor other activities if paid employment dominates their entire existence.

All of this should not really need saying. Life should not consist of a forced choice between unlimited hours of work and "other" activities. There *are* reasons to reduce work obligations other than the need to care for small children: elderly relatives need care as well, and someone has to volunteer for the charitable organizations that are often invoked as alternatives to the welfare state. Not least, people simply enjoy work more, and often work better, when they have a degree of control over its scheduling.

Unfortunately, all of these reminders remain necessary. As Joan Williams (2000) argues, the "ideal worker norm" of intensive and extensive work remains pervasive and reduced work options remain marginalized, even stigmatized. The idea that one can combine gratifying paid employment with other activities, as our respondents are attempting to do, sounds farfetched, utopian, beyond the reach of all but the luckiest individuals. Family-friendly policies do not even try to produce this combination; instead, they remain within the logic that treats "life" as a hyphenated add-on to "work." They are typically intended to allow people (and a limited group at that) to "survive" the demands of family so that they can eventually return to work, as it is ordinarily understood. American culture continues to portray paid employment and "leisure" as an either/or proposition. The cultural right still dreams of a family life that never existed, with stay-at-home moms spending their time at the PTA and church volunteer groups, a world in which gender is the dividing line between work and everything else. Elsewhere, however, this vision has almost completely given way to a definition of work as an obligation for all, as the only legitimate way to participate meaningfully in social life. Women who reduce their hours at work for family reasons are seen as "making sacrifices"; men who reduce their hours at work, for whatever reason, are almost incomprehensible.

The terms in which work time is debated are so limited that part-time work earns little respect. It is often portrayed as a second-rate option seized by people who cannot get full-time jobs, or as a source of pin money. Even good part-time jobs of the kind we have discussed here are criticized for catering only to women, who must sacrifice their careers to meet society's expectations. As our respondents testify, this is much too limited a frame for thinking about hours at work. They regard work as an activity that can and should be combined with other activities in a set of arrangements customized to suit the needs of specific individuals.

When we speak in public about our research, we are often asked how we defined part-time. We didn't. We simply asked the people we talked with if they were deliberately reducing their paid work time to pursue some other agenda. What is important is not the number of hours they work—from 25 to 40 hours per week on average—but their ability to arrange those hours to suit their needs. A three-day week allows some respondents to spend the time that they want with their children. Others want to work during school hours. Some, usually independent contractors, arrange to take long breaks from work, either to cover school vacations or to travel. Some see a reduction in hours as a short-term expedient to cover a temporary need; others, whether by design or not, have come to see it as a more permanent option. What they all have in common—women and men, young and old—is that they are chipping away at the conventional view of the ideal worker, one who works full-time for the organization.

This chipping away is usually an individual activity, something each feels privileged to enjoy. Nonetheless, we can learn from their experience what it would it take to make such customization available to a broader range of people. Most directly, we can learn what is possible under prevailing circumstances. Our respondents have found ways to circumvent the ideal worker norm that actually work. If we examine the practical arrangements they make and the resources they make use of, we can begin to develop a guide to how other individuals might follow suit. Taking a broader view, we can also learn much by looking at the structural problems that make part-time work sometimes costly and difficult to obtain. For customized work to become truly acceptable and available to all, it will be necessary to go beyond individual solutions to examine the larger social conditions that define and support the ideal worker norm.

Practical Arrangements

Much of what our respondents told us indicates that there is substantial leeway, either within organizations or in the market for contractors, for individuals to carve out alternative work schedules. Since these arrangements are often a matter of individual initiative, it may be useful to summarize their information about strategies that work.

Working Part-Time for an Organization

- *Do not assume that an organization's policy faithfully reflects what is possible.*

Many organizations have no formal policy allowing for reduced work schedules. The lack of a policy does not mean that it is impossible to arrange such a schedule, as several of our respondents discovered. Perhaps no one has given any thought to the matter. Perhaps management is reluctant to encourage requests. Whatever the reason, it may be possible to work something out in the absence of a policy if one asks. Indeed, some technical professionals feel that lack of a policy is an advantage: a policy can be unnecessarily limiting, and managers may use it as an excuse to deny the precise reconfiguration of time that an employee wants. Even if the organization does have a formal policy, it is often ignored. A formal policy may mask management's reluctance to implement it. Conversely, a policy specifying the forms reduced work schedules may take may be bent to accommodate employees whom management wants to accommodate. Individuals seeking reduced work arrangements should assume that they are starting from scratch. The task of arranging a part-time schedule is one of negotiation and persuasion, not a simple matter of pointing to a policy that authorizes what you want.

- *Find an agreeable manager.*

In part because formal policies are poor guides to what is possible, it is also important for prospective part-timers to find an agreeable manager. Whether or not an organization has a formal policy in respect to part-time work, individual managers vary tremendously in their willingness to accommodate employees who want to reduce their work hours. Fortunately, it is often possible to move laterally in organizations, to shift across departments or units in search of congenial work arrangements. Several of the people with whom we spoke have followed precisely this procedure, and recommend it if your supervisor is not supportive of your request to reduce your work schedule.

- *Work with colleagues to solve scheduling problems.*

Making part-time schedules work is greatly helped by the cooperation of colleagues. We heard numerous stories about the role of colleagues—both about colleagues who grumble and snipe at people who work part-time and about those who are supportive and accommodating.[1] Aside from the obvious fact that supportive colleagues make the workplace far more pleasant for everyone, part-

---

1. Some writers on part-time work contend that nonparents resent the "privileges" bestowed upon working parents by "family-friendly" policies. See Burkett (2000) for an example of this genre.

timers' colleagues can be either resources or obstacles in work-places where teamwork and cooperation are the norm. If they insist on scheduling meetings at awkward times, if they demand that work be completed on a schedule that makes part-time work im-practical, conflicts are inevitable. If, on the other hand, they try to be helpful, colleagues can make part-time work possible by doing things like pinch-hitting for a part-timer who cannot attend an in-conveniently scheduled meeting or accepting time-consuming jobs that the part-timer finds it difficult to take on.

So what can you do to encourage cooperation from colleagues?

- *Be accessible.*

Many of our respondents talked about the efforts they make to re-main accessible, even when they are not officially at work. They in-vite colleagues and clients to call them at home, respond promptly to messages and requests left for them, and make extensive use of e-mail and other electronic media to maintain contact and regular communi-cation. This strategy deals directly with one of the primary objections to working with people who are on a reduced schedule—that they are not there when you need them. In effect, part-timers find ways to be there even when they are not physically present; at least, enough to mute the criticism that their absence is holding up the work process.

- *Do face work.*

It is important to create the impression of being at work as much as possible. The co-workers of some of our respondents are unaware that they are actually working part-time. In most workplaces, people are away from their work stations from time to time during the day, so that it can be difficult to know who is actually at work and who is not. Part-timers find that they can take advantage of this situation by making sure that others are always aware of their pres-ence when they are actually at work. They make a deliberate effort to be visible: they draw attention to themselves by announcing their presence, greeting fellow workers, dropping in on significant co-workers and supervisors. As long as one also does one's job, this strategy is often enough to create the impression that an employee is there at all times.

- *Do good work.*

Implicit in what we have just said is the necessity of doing a good job. Most part-time professionals take considerable pride in their ability to do their jobs well as part-timers. Their satisfaction in a job well done is not only a matter of their commitment to work, it is also an important part of sustaining reduced work arrangements. A part-timer who holds up the work flow or does less than high-quality work is obviously vulnerable to criticism from hostile colleagues and supervisors. As a result, many of the people with whom we spoke emphasize the importance of getting your work done, getting it done on time, and getting it done well.

- *Make yourself a valued employee.*

The chance of successfully negotiating these arrangements is enhanced if one is a valued employee. Many organizations regard part-time work as a reward to loyal employees whom they wish to retain. As a result, it is usually difficult for newer employees to get desirable part-time jobs; and it is uncommon for organizations to fill desirable positions with people who say that they want to work part-time. Tactically, then, people who want to reduce their work hours are obliged to wait until they have established themselves as deserving of this kind of treatment, perhaps by developing a highly desirable set of skills.

- *Make use of the situations assumed to justify a request for part-time work.*

Some reasons offered for asking for part-time work are socially approved and recognized as valid by the organization. Most of the people we spoke with said that when women ask for part-time work on the grounds that they have small children at home, employers are likely to treat the request as legitimate. They may not automatically say yes, but they acknowledge the appropriateness of a mother's desire to spend time caring for her children. This motivation is far less available to men. Our respondents tell us that they believe their employers do not think the same way about fathers as about mothers. So male part-time employees tend to use other justifications for their requests: partial retirement (an option open to women as well, in principle, but few female technical professionals are approaching retirement age) or a desire for additional education. In general, it helps if an individual can identify a reason for wanting part-time work that fits social and organizational views of who they are. It also helps to tie the desire for part-time work to, say, improving performance, or to suggest that it might help employee retention.

- *You're not alone—talk to others.*

Several part-timers with whom we spoke described themselves as having initiated their discussion of reducing their work hours without really knowing how it might be done or whether others had done it before them. They described their lack of awareness as a problem. Some of them discovered later on that other employees were in a similar situation, and that discussing things with them helped them make their schedules work. A few workplaces have established support groups for actual or prospective part-time workers, and our respondents found that these mechanisms really helped make things easier for people considering part-time options. Other people told us how important it had been to them to learn of someone who had taken the same route before them. They sought out that person, asked for information, and used what they learned in preparing to ask for reduced work arrangements of their own. The message in all of these stories is that, particularly in a workplace where part-time schedules must be negotiated individually, having information about what others have done can serve both as ammunition and as a guide to what to ask for, and how.

Contracting

Contractors, too, told us about strategies that work. Some of them are quite similar to those described by employees, but others are specific to the situation of contractors:

- *Be available.*

Like organizational professionals, independent contractors emphasized the importance of creating the impression of availability so that clients will not find their part-time status to be an inconvenience or assume that they must be scheduled so far in advance that it's impractical to consider them. Many make a practice of giving out their home phone numbers, taking work calls outside of normal (for them) work hours, and responding to electronic communications at odd hours. Several part-timers who work at home told us that they conceal from their clients the fact that they work at home; they try to create the impression that they are in an office when they interact with clients. Like organizational professionals, contractors talk about making themselves visible to the people with whom they work. To fit the expectations of their clients, some make visits to work sites that they feel are not really necessary to the work. We also heard from several contractors who echo organizational employees' emphasis on doing face work when they are on site: they make sure that people notice them so that a clear memory of their presence is created. These strategies, like those employed by part-time employees, are designed to neutralize the anticipated criticism of their unavailability at crucial points in the work cycle.

- *Develop a reputation for doing good work.*

Contractors consistently told us that a reputation for doing good work is crucial to ensuring the flow of work that they need; they also told us that it helps them to gain the autonomy they desire. The people we interviewed work consciously at creating a good reputation. When they have a new client, they make a point of doing a particularly good job, sometimes bidding low to create a reputation for providing a low-cost service. With established clients, they strive to deliver the quality of service for which they have become known and attempt to beat deadlines, both to create a good impression and to avoid scrutiny. Most of the contractors find that their clients do not attempt to scrutinize their day-to-day activities very closely. As long as they do the work well, deliver it on time, and communicate effectively, they are able to maintain a high level of autonomy, allowing them greater freedom to work as they want and when they want.

• *Develop a network.*

Most contractors also stress the importance of developing a network. The most reliable, consistent source of work, they find, is a network of clients and colleagues who can refer work to them. The most established of the contractors we met told us that, more often than not, work comes to them (rather than having to be sought out) through their network. Networks also allow contractors to farm out work to other independents if they have too much work and do not want to turn down potentially valuable clients.

• *Minimize nonbillable hours.*

One of the biggest problems independent contractors face is spending time doing work for which they do not get paid: soliciting business by making calls, researching local markets to identify potential customers, attending meetings, going to trade shows. Most technical professionals dislike this kind of activity, in part because it is not the technical work they enjoy, in part because it is unpaid, in part because the time spent on it is infinitely expandable. If one wants to, one can spend enormous amounts of time beating the bushes for business. Successful part-time contractors suggest that reducing the time spent on these activities is the most important way to maintain control of one's hours of work. Ideally, they hope to be able to do none of this sort of work, relying instead on networks and referrals for a steady, manageable flow of business.

• *Learn how to estimate how long jobs will take and how much they will cost.*

Contractors also emphasize the importance of making realistic bids on the jobs for which they contract. Many tell of mistakes they made early in their careers as contractors by grossly underbidding on jobs to get business, only to discover either that they did not make any money on the job or that they had to spend far more time on it than they had anticipated—thus, of course, undermining their control over their time. As they gained experience, they learned how to bid accurately on jobs, to make realistic assessments of how long a job will actually take, to build cushions into their bids to allow for unanticipated complications and to compensate for non-billable time that is nevertheless a necessary part of getting the job done. Again, the object is to achieve control over one's work time; mastering the bidding process proves to be an important step in doing so.

Domestic Arrangements

Finally, we learned from our respondents about the importance of working things out at home.

- *Assert control over your time at home.*

One of the complaints we heard most frequently concerns other people's attitudes toward their time. Many told us that friends and relatives assume that when they are home they are available to take people to the airport, run errands, mind children, or simply visit. Part-timers experience these intrusions as assaults on the time arrangements they are attempting to construct. Those who actually work at home resent the assumption that people at home are not working. Even those who do not work at home voice the same complaints; they have reduced their work hours to free some time for other enjoyable activities (child care, hobbies, education, volunteer work), not to become caught up in doing things imposed upon them by others. While no one has found a foolproof solution to this problem, all emphasize the importance of avoiding the trap produced by others' assumption that a person at home is always available to them.

- *Don't get caught up in housework.*

A specific version of the concern over controlling one's domestic time comes from the mothers with whom we spoke. They, too, encounter demanding relatives and needy neighbors, but they are more likely to talk about the danger of becoming consumed by domestic labor. As we have seen, many experience at least a partial reassertion of unequal domestic gender roles after they decide to work part-time. Their husbands assume that because they spend more time at home than they used to, they can and should shoulder the burden of housework. Some also admit they are their own worst enemy in this regard; they find themselves doing more domestic labor than they had done as full-timers because they are now at home and can see things that need to be done.

Few are happy with this situation; most take one or more partially effective steps to change it. A few women openly confront their husbands, demanding that they do a larger share of the domestic labor. Others resort to subtler methods, such as defining certain times as dad's time to be with the kids (often Saturdays), then attaching other domestic responsibilities to this time ("Take the kids shopping"). Most commonly, however, the women we met deal with the problem by resisting their tendency (if they have one) to do more by hiring a cleaner and purchasing prepared food. While we met few women who live in what could be described as egalitarian households, we also met very few who complained of being overwhelmed by housework.

Structural Impediments and Social Change

All this advice is directed to individuals and it is as individuals that the people we talked with manage to customize their own work time. But often they achieve their success only because of the particular circumstances that allow them to overcome broader structural impediments, or because they are able and willing to pay the costs associated with most customized work. If customized work is to be extended, we need to look more closely at some of these impediments and costs, and seek ways to minimize or eliminate them.

Income and Benefits

Among the most obvious problems is the economic loss that part-time work entails. As one would expect, all the part-timers and independent contractors we spoke with had their income reduced when they cut back on their hours, in some cases quite dramatically because of a change in job classification or work arrangements. They also have generally experienced a reduction or absolute loss of benefits. Independent contractors need to allocate a larger percentage of their income to health insurance and retirement savings. Our respondents earn solid middle-class incomes and are comfortable economically, but the loss of income is real.

The fact that these economic consequences are not more significant for our respondents is a function of their social situation. They are mainly middle-class professionals married to other affluent professionals and managers, so their family incomes are usually high enough to absorb the losses reduced work arrangements generally entail. People with more modest incomes, especially those not married to high earners, are not in a position to give up income and benefits in this way.

A reduction in income remains the most stubborn obstacle to a reduction in work time, especially for people whose incomes have not kept up with those of professional and managerial employees. The emerging "simple living" movement may help to undercut the consumerism that has been central to the postwar American dream, but a society dependent on private solutions to day care, retirement, college, and transportation costs places strict limits on the expenditures many middle- and low-income Americans can cut from their budgets.[2] Many of the economic problems would be taken off the table were the United States to provide benefits and income supports of the kind common in Western Europe. The prospects of such legislation are so slim, however, that high earnings are likely to remain a necessary condition for choosing to reduce one's hours for most Americans.

Careers

The possibilities look more hopeful for another of the costs associated with part-time work: the negative career consequences of working reduced hours. While some of the corporate part-timers do suggest that their chances for promotion have been unaffected by their move to part-time work, more feel that their chances for mobility have been either put on hold or permanently damaged, particularly their chances of moving into management. Although techni-

---

2. See Schor 1998 for an argument that excess consumerism is a partial source of Americans' time crunch.

cal professionals' ambivalence about managerial roles often mutes any sense of loss, part-time work does continue to be associated with delayed or blocked mobility.

Nonetheless, while part-time work may mean settling for second best in the world of New York corporate lawyers, it is not the case here. Our respondents show that interesting and important technical work can be done on a part-time basis, whether one works directly for a company or as an independent contractor. Even lower levels of the management hierarchy can be managed, especially as a job-share. The work they do give up is the least interesting. They miss meetings, but few technical professionals come home from work complaining of missing a great meeting. Technical career structures are changing, creating more satisfactory and responsible work at the practitioner level without resort to the bureaucratic advancement that is the sine qua non for success in other jobs. Nor does taking part-time work imply giving up the possibility of returning to a career later. Technical professionals can maintain their high-demand skills while working part-time and are paid well. They are not like women who sacrifice career for family and twenty years later find themselves totally dependent on their husbands for support. This may be part-time work, but it is good work.

The structure of technical careers, with its discontinuity between bureaucratic career success and technical fulfillment, is part of the story. Technical professionals have always been ambivalent about their orientation: they enjoy the technical practice that drew them into the profession in the first place but are motivated to climb the corporate ladder into management by the offer of rewards and privileges. Employers have always manipulated this dual orientation. When they want to encourage a bureaucratic orientation in their engineers, they routinely structure rewards to encourage it. When they want to focus on technical performance, the reward structure is reengineered to produce that result (Whalley 1986b). In recent years there has been a move away from the bureaucratic structure toward reliance on the external labor market, as seen in the decline of IBM and the rise of Silicon Valley as the image of the labor market for technical professionals.

This renewed occupationalization has advantages for the development of customized work. In part, reliance on external recruitment and the formation and reconfiguration of project teams place the emphasis on expertise rather than demonstrated organizational experience. It is easier for workers with unorthodox time schedules to demonstrate expertise rather than organizational commitment. Second, as loyalty has become more tenuous in companies that rely on project teams, which often include contractors, it has come to play a less powerful role in employers' rhetoric, although it still figures prominently in managers' talk about the allocation of part-time work. The presence of part-timers looks less unusual in a team made up of relative newcomers than in a department where organizational commitment is on conspicuous display. Third, the use of independent contractors provides an ever-present alternative model of good work being done under conditions that differ from those of the traditional employment package. Without wishing to denigrate in any way the importance of removing the glass ceiling that impedes women's rise to the very top of organizations, we must acknowledge that many, perhaps most, technical professionals, men and women, are content with a decent job, with reasonable prospects and the time to enjoy other activities as well.

Can these conditions of technical work serve as a model for other occupations? In many ways, modern engineering has some of the characteristics of nursing and teaching, two traditionally female-friendly occupations with interesting work, short career ladders, and flexible hours. Technical professions, however, have higher prestige and much higher pay, though history might lead a pessimist to worry about the consequences for both if there were an influx of women. Nonetheless, the focus on interesting work at decent pay does fit more closely with what many people want out of work than the excessive time commitment demanded by the traditional bureaucracy. The restructuring of organizations away from extended ranks of middle management, the increased talk of flexibility, and the reliance on structures of normative commitment rather than direct supervision, all suggest that some of these conditions may be extended to other corporate professionals.

What the people we talked with are seeking is the equivalent of flexible production. Just as companies have increasingly tried to tailor their production efforts to meet their output needs, so employees want the opportunity to tailor their time at work. As companies are finding out in other areas, flexibility sometimes means doing away with centralized standards. Formal human relations policies that spell out rules and regulations for part-time work often get in the way of the customized work arrangements that people want. A fixed limit on the length of time an employee can work part-time and regulations that tie benefits to the number of hours worked can both create problems.

Employers have long insisted that in return for the privilege of exempt status, they have a right to demand "reasonable" flexibility: no overtime pay, no rigid adherence to the clock. The employees we heard from are asking for similar flexibility. It is a flexibility that employers often find it easier to grant independent contractors, since by law they are able to demand only output, not the way the output is delivered. Employees would like the same kind of flexibility.

The computerization of employee records ought to make this kind of thing easier, just as it has facilitated flexible and just-in-time production. To achieve flexibility, however, employers would have to accept the proposition that employees who want to reduce their work hours may be just as committed to the organization's goals as full-time workers. As Gideon Kunda and others have shown, employers of technical professionals increasingly rely on internalized normative commitment, rather than direct supervision, as a mechanism of managerial control (Kunda 1992, Gibbon and al. 1994). The technical professionals we heard from, contractors and employees alike, showed a very high level of commitment to getting the job done, and done well. If employers could move away from the equation of face time with commitment, a major barrier to more widespread customization would be removed.

From the individual's point of view, a lifelong series of choices has to be made: how long to work and for whom; whether to take a full-time job or be independent; what skills are worth investing in. As we discovered when we found that we could not clearly demarcate occupational identities, this career strategy is highly individualized; one cannot simply become an engineer, just as one can no longer be an IBMer. What matters is the particular skills and experiences one brings to a specific job transaction. Customizing work time is the logical extension of this individualization of bargaining in the labor market.

Gender

Even if customized work becomes widely available, it will still be problematic if it remains highly gendered. We must acknowledge the argument made by many feminist scholars, that part-time work is often a gender trap, a way to preserve a traditional gendered division of labor. According to this view, part-time work gets men off the hook by making it possible for their wives to look after children and do the household labor while still contributing to the household income, thus reinforcing the idea that this division of labor is normative and preventing the kind of true sharing that is held up as the ideal.[3]

It is true that the choice of part-time work is currently heavily gendered. Even after an intensive search, we found few men customizing their work time, and we found nothing to suggest that our sample is unusual in this respect. Our study suggests, however, that the other elements of this critique are not so well founded.

We have already indicated that even the mothers we talked with are not sacrificing their lives on the altar of domesticity. We heard from no budding interior decorators or gourmet cooks, no moms dreaming of the 1950s. All they want is a reasonable workday, the kind of workday common in European societies, where long hours are likely to be seen as evidence of incompetence rather than testimony to hard work and commitment. With the extra time, they want to be with their children. We heard from women who enjoy parenting, love it in fact, but do not feel compelled to do it full-time. They feel comfortable, even relieved, to be sharing the responsibilities of child care with friends, family, or day care providers, at least some of the time. They feel they can be perfectly satisfactory parents without embracing any cultural expectation of intensive mothering. We did not hear these women talking about parenting as an obligation and work as self-gratification, a convention that only feeds into stereotypes of the "selfless" woman and the "self-fulfilled" man. Repeatedly we heard them talk about their

---

3. See Deutsch 1999 for an account that emphasizes equal sharing. Deutsch does acknowledge, as some do not, that equal sharing of unreasonable work loads liberates no one. She advocates both sharing and more flexible work hours for men and women, a goal many of our respondents would certainly endorse.

children in the same terms they use to talk about their work, as a source of intense personal satisfaction. We also heard them say that they have reduced their work time for their own benefit, not because their husbands would not do their fair share of parenting and housework. It is true that by working part-time these women enable their husbands to focus on full-time careers and minimize their family commitments, but rather than feeling like victims, many of these women pity their husbands for missing out on the joys of parenting.

The success of this strategy owes much to the fact that these women have reconstructed the traditional housewife package along with the professional package. At work they have minimized what they see as the least satisfying aspects of their jobs but kept the core of satisfying work; at home they try to minimize the domestic labor they find onerous and maximize the time they spend with their children, the most satisfying part of the domestic package to them. They want to be moms, not housewives. They are following what Anthony Giddens (1991) considers a characteristic feature of late modernity, the "self-construction" of identities. Rather than "finding themselves" in one of Kathleen Gerson's (1985) "hard choices" between work and home, these women are creating themselves in a lifelong process of reflection on all the various aspects of social life that they no longer take for granted. They are living out what might be called a new identity narrative, a pattern we can see most clearly in the process by which they first decide to customize their work time and then decide to continue doing so.

It is not surprising that women have been at the forefront of self-reflection and the challenging of traditional practices and identities. Even the most conservative and traditional woman could not have missed the public discourse over the remaking of women's roles. This process opens up possibilities for men, too, since traditional patterns of gender relation can no longer be taken for granted (Beck 1992). Particularly if domestic labor ceases to be so onerous and time-consuming, and if it comes to be associated with those aspects of domestic life that are genuinely rewarding, it is not hard to imagine that more men may find the option of reducing work to make room for domestic life attractive.

However, to dismiss as irrelevant the continued gendered nature of many of these developments would also be a mistake. If the kind of customized work arrangements we have been discussing remain an option for women only, there is a real danger that they could become the mommy track that critics already insist they are. If they become routine for women but not for men, they could provide a rationale—though, as we have seen, not a justification—for sidelining women into less interesting jobs and maintaining the glass ceiling. Similarly, on the domestic front, if only women free up time to be at home, they will continue to be held solely responsible for parenting and domestic labor.

There is some evidence, however, that changing gender patterns may increase access to part-time work for both women and men. Research on male workers finds an increase in interest in family and in willingness to share domestic and child care responsibilities.[4] Younger workers appear to be less dedicated to long-term careers than those in generations past. We did hear from a few men who had chosen to work part-time while raising a family. In some ways, these men do appear to have embraced a different definition of work commitment. Yet they remain ambivalent about their situation in ways that reveal some of the obstacles to a serious challenge to existing professional work arrangements.

John, an engineer whose wife also works part-time at the same company, remains ambivalent about traditional male notions of career. He expresses both optimism and pessimism about the degree to which corporate attitudes to part-time work are changing. He seems torn between accepting the idea that moving up the corporate ladder is not important and hoping that attitudes will change enough to allow mobility for part-timers as well:

> Well, you know, from a philosophical point of view, things are changing, O.K. When I started eighteen years ago, there was no one working part-time. When I initially was promoted, say ten or eleven years ago, there were people working part-time, but there were not any technical managers part-time. So who's to say, within the next ten years, maybe there'll be some part-time department heads. You know, right now, that does not seem very probable, but eighteen years ago, anybody working part-time here didn't seem very probable either.

4. See the work reported in Pleck 1993, Coltrane 1996, Barnett and Rivers 1996, Tilly 1996, and Robinson and Godbey 1997.

At the same time, John also appears to have reconciled himself to part-time status because he sees his career prospects as poor:

> Rightly or wrongly, as far as working full-time, I would never get promoted to the next level. I mean, I just, I see people who are getting promoted, and they have skills that I don't have. I need to be more, more aggressive, and I've been a supervisor for ten or eleven years, and I don't see myself getting promoted to the next level. So it wasn't an issue of . . . will this change my career.

Thus John has not completely abandoned the traditional male definition of career, although he has clearly moved some way beyond it. He is at least able to reconcile himself to his situation as a part-time worker and values the family life it has made possible. In this reconciliation, however, we can see an element of sour grapes, a feeling that John is sacrificing something he wanted but could not have under any circumstances. Many men and women in corporations are likely to be in this situation—plateaued, regretful about their careers, and open to alternative definitions of work commitment and alternative sources of personal satisfaction.

If more men move toward the part-time option, the possibilities of a broader customization of work time will increase, but it matters whether the men involved are like this engineer or not. If men in general begin to accept part-time work, employers will be faced with a general challenge to the currently rigid structures of work. If, however, all the men who choose part-time work are perceived to have gone as far as they can go, then part-time work may remain stigmatized, at least for men. As we have suggested, the next revolution may be to change the culture of men rather than to stigmatize women for wanting something more than work.

A Social Movement?

At the heart of the problem with extending customized work time is the continued perception that to reduce one's work time is to be deviant. Many employers use time demands as a way to measure loyalty and competence; they ration opportunities for part-time work, reserving them for a select few employees whom they fear to lose. Moreover, managers' perception that part-timers are not full members of the corporate culture helps block their promotion chances. Even many of the strategies that individuals develop to maximize their flexibility—concealing the fact that they work part-time, making themselves ever available, and so on—can reinforce resistance, since such strategies reinforce the idea that the normal workweek is at least 40 hours long. The continued marginalization of part-time work also gives employers some leverage to use in demanding additional work; the part-timers feel lucky to have been given "special" treatment and feel some pressure to keep up with their full-time colleagues.

It is to challenge this sense of individual deviance that part-timers insist on the importance of talking to and learning from others. A network of part-timers, who tell one another about what is possible, support one another by indicating that they are not alone, and disseminate information about part-time options, is a powerful mechanism for increasing the possibilities. As we talked with part-timers about their experiences, we sometimes had the impression that an incipient social movement is gathering around reduced work options. People seem to be trying to develop networks that promote the idea of reduced work time. If this idea becomes more general and merges with the increasing emphasis on downshifting to make time for the things people find more satisfying than the corporate lockstep, employers may find that they have no choice but to facilitate the customization of work schedules.

The people we heard from are not public revolutionaries, and probably are not typical of the vast majority of part-time employees. They have interesting jobs, decent pay, and often family support. In the shaping of social change, however, it is not always the most typical who have the most impact. In fact, the privileges of the people we studied are what permit them to explore new ways of doing things. Because their jobs are interesting, they can retain a professional commitment to work apart from the company that employs them. Because their skills are transferable, they can belong to networks of fellow professionals even without becoming independent contractors, while the existence of a flourishing independent network creates opportunities unavailable to those whose skills are bound to the organization. Their stable finances allow them to reduce their income without suffering too much and still allow them to rely on the market for those resources they are comfortable purchasing. In the struggle to customize work time, as in so many other endeavors, it is those with the security of privilege who can afford to take the risks, to carve out new strategies, and, most important, to lay down a track for others to follow.

Though we talk of privilege, these are not the high-tech millionaires of the two coasts or the in-demand hot professionals whose stories makes good leads for the media. Their privileges are relative: relative only to those with uninteresting jobs in low demand, whose incomes imply a perpetual struggle. In many other ways our respondents are representative of the American middle class. They are representative enough, in any case, to be role models for large numbers of people who might want to follow their example. Having spent our careers in the Midwest, we are tempted to argue, too, that they are more representative of a broad swath of Americans than New Yorkers or the denizens of Silicon Valley. A Cornell research team once tentatively suggested that their upstate New York sample might be less driven to work because they live in a rural setting; that urban settings—they cite Chicago as an example—may be different (Becker and Moen 1998). We found that committed, hardworking, good technical professionals in Cleveland and Chicago— the third-largest high-tech center in the country—also show that there can be more to life than work.

The workplace is structured around a view of professional identity that assumes it is all-consuming; chosen at an early age, inculcated in professional school, dominating one's life course and one's life. But this view no longer fits the way our respondents want to live. They view their careers as emergent and changing, a view that leaves them free to make choices about the direction their work should take and the time it should consume. They want to feel free to perform and possess multiple identities—engineer, mom, environmentalist. To do so, however, they must challenge institutions that demand that they subsume all identities under one— parent, retiree, or professional.

Although it will require work, the satisfaction we heard from the women and men we talked with suggests that reducing the demands of a greedy work organization doesn't require one to give up the satisfactions of work, it simply allows time for other things. To spend more time with one's children is not to surrender to an oppressive ideology; parenting can be satisfying work, too. The rigidities of the institutional mapping of work as an occupation for men and family as an occupation for women are breaking down. Women may have been at the forefront of these changes because it is their identities that have been most radically reconstituted in the last half-century, but the changes pioneered by the people we talked with have extended the range of choices open to everyone.

Appendix

Interview Agenda

Although we did not make use of a detailed interview schedule, we were concerned to touch on the same topics with all interviewees, so we used the following agenda to shape discussion.

1. How did the interviewee come to be a part-time worker? What was his or her specific personal experience? In what sense was the arrangement voluntary? Did the employer do anything to make the transition from full-time staff employment easier or more convenient? Was the choice of part-time work in any way forced by actions of the employer? Was the choice in some way constrained or facilitated by family or other circumstances?

2. How does the labor market operate for part-time and contingent or flexible workers? How do these workers find jobs? How do employers find appropriate workers? Do such workers typically stay attached to one employer, or do they shift from employer to employer? If the latter, how do they identify job opportunities? How is market information developed and disseminated, so that consultants, the self-employed, and independent contractors can secure work and become known to employers? What role do networks and formal job placement agencies play in the labor market for this kind of employment? Is it difficult to obtain appropriate kinds of part-time employment or to maintain flexibility in other kinds of employment? What are the difficulties, if any?

3. How do the careers of such workers evolve? What has been the

career pattern of individual workers to date and how do they envisage their future careers? Do workers typically go from full-time employment to part-time work? Is part-time work a probationary prelude to a full-time staff position? Do workers move in and out of part-time work as their life circumstances and employment opportunities change? Do part-time workers move in and out of temporary employment, self-employment, or some other form of contingent work? Have they encountered structural barriers to any type of contingent work? Have the experiences of men and women differed in ways that channel them into different kinds of jobs? How do they structure their résumés in such circumstances? Do employers develop distinctive flexible career tracks to accommodate such workers?

4. Does working fewer than regular hours affect the terms and conditions of employment? Does it lower income? Are there circumstances in which income is raised? Do all workers lose benefits? If so, are they able to find alternatives? Does a desire for flexibility cause income and employment to become noticeably more insecure? Are there times when work is hard to obtain? Does the choice of part-time employment have any effect on the content of work—that is, on the specific types of work the individual performs? Are these changes, if any, positive or not?

5. How are relationships with employers affected by part-time or independent status? How does the employer or client control and supervise the work such people do? What kinds of legal relationship develop between such workers and their employers or clients? Does working other than regular hours give the worker more or less autonomy? How do employers deal with the difficulties of overseeing work done at home? How do such workers ensure that they are adequately compensated for their work? How are the difficult issues of intellectual property dealt with in these newly developing employment relationships?

6. How does such employment affect the part of technical workers' work lives for which they are not paid? Does part-time work enable them to balance their domestic and work obligations to their own satisfaction? If not, why not? What changes in the typical part-time work arrangement might improve this balance? Does the choice of part-time work create new problems that workers had not anticipated? If workers have household partners, how did they negotiate the decision to work part-time, and how has it affected their financial relationship? How have their friends and colleagues reacted to their decision?

References

Aronowitz, Stanley, and William Difazio. 1995. *The Jobless Future: Sci-Tech and the Dogma of Work.* Minneapolis: University of Minnesota Press.

Arthur, M. B., and D. M. Rousseau. 1996. *The Boundaryless Career: New Employment Principles for a New Organizational Era.* New York: Oxford University Press.

Bailyn, Lotte. 1993. *Breaking the Mold: Women, Men, and Time in the New Corporate World.* New York: Free Press.

Barley, Stephen R. 1991. "The New Crafts: On the Technicization of the Workforce and the Occupationalization of Firms." University of Pennsylvania/National Center for the Education of the Workforce.

Barnett, Rosalind, and Caryl Rivers. 1996. *He Works, She Works.* New York: HarperCollins.

Beck, Ulrich. 1992. *Risk Society.* Trans. M. Ritter. London: Sage.

Becker, Howard. 1960. "Notes on the Concept of Commitment." *American Journal of Sociology* 66:32–40.

Becker, Penny Edgell, and Phyllis Moen. 1999. "Scaling Back: Dual-Earner Couples' Work-Family Strategies." *Journal of Marriage and the Family* 61: 995–1007.

Beechey, Veronica, and Tessa Perkins. 1987. *A Matter of Hours: Women, Part-Time Work, and the Labor Market.* Minneapolis: University of Minnesota Press.

Belous, Richard. 1989. "How Human Resource Systems Adjust to the Shift Towards Contingent Workers." *Monthly Labor Review* 112:7–12.

Bielby, Denise, and William T. Bielby. 1988. "Women's and Men's Commitment to Paid Work and Family: Theories, Models, and Hypotheses." In *Women and Work: An Annual Review,* vol. 3, ed. B. Gutek, A. Stromberg, and L. Larwood. Newbury Park, Calif.: Sage.

Blank, Rebecca. 1989. "The Role of Part-Time Work in Women's Labor Market Choices over Time." *American Economic Review* 70:295–99.

Brint, Steven. 1994. *In an Age of Experts*. Princeton: Princeton University Press.

Burkett, Elinor. 2000. *The Baby Boon: How Family-Friendly America Cheats the Childless*. New York: Free Press.

Butler, Judith. 1990. *Gender Trouble*. New York: Routledge.

Christensen, Kathleen. 1988. "Introduction: White Collar Home-Based Work." In *The New Era of Home-Based Work: Directions and Policies*, ed. K. Christensen. Boulder: Westview.

——. 1989. "Flexible Staffing and Scheduling in U.S. Corporations." Conference Board, New York.

Clarkberg, Marin, and Phyllis Moen. 1998. "Working Families in Transition: Husbands' and Wives' Hours on the Job." Cornell Employment and Family Careers Institute, Ithaca, N.Y.

Cohen, Laurie, and Mary Mallon. 1999. "The Transition from Organizational Employment to Portfolio Working: Perceptions of 'Boundarylessness.'" *Work, Employment, and Society* 13:329–52.

Coltrane, Scott. 1996. *Family Man: Fatherhood, Housework, and Gender Equity*. New York: Oxford University Press.

Coser, Lewis. 1974. *Greedy Institutions: Patterns of Undivided Commitment*. New York: Free Press.

Daniels, Arlene. 1988. *Invisible Careers: Women Civic Leaders from the Volunteer World*. Chicago: University of Chicago Press.

Deutsch, Francine. 1999. *Halving It All: How Equally Shared Parenting Works*. Cambridge: Harvard University Press.

DeVault, Marjorie. 1990. "Talking and Listening from Women's Standpoint: Feminist Strategies for Interviewing and Analysis." *Social Problems* 37:96–116.

——. 1994. *Feeding the Family: The Social Organization of Caring as Gendered Work*. Chicago: University of Chicago Press.

DiTomaso, Nancy. 1996. "The Loose Coupling of Jobs: The Subcontracting of Everyone." Paper presented at the annual meeting of the American Sociological Association, New York.

Doeringer, Peter, ed. 1990. *Bridges to Retirement: Older Workers in a Changing Labor Market*. Ithaca: ILR Press.

Ehrenreich, Barbara. 1995. "In Search of a Simpler Life." *Working Woman*, December, pp. 27–29,62.

Epstein, Cynthia, Carroll Seron, Bonnie Oglensky, and Robert Sauté. 1999. *The Part-Time Paradox: Time Norms, Professional Life, Family, and Gender*. New York: Routledge.

Evetts, Julia. 1996. *Gender and Career in Science and Engineering*. London: Taylor & Francis.

Fried, Mindy. 1998. *Taking Time: Parental Leave Policy and Corporate Culture*. Philadelphia: Temple University Press.

Galinsky, Ellen. 1999. *Ask the Children: What America's Children Really Think about Working*. New York: Morrow.

Garey, Anita Ilta. 1999. *Weaving Work and Motherhood*. Philadelphia: Temple University Press.

Gerson, Kathleen. 1985. *Hard Choices: How Women Decide about Work, Career, and Motherhood*. Berkeley: University of California Press.

Gibbon, Michael, et al. 1994. *The New Production of Knowledge: The Dynamics of Science and Research in Contemporary Societies*. London: Sage.

Giddens, Anthony. 1991. *Modernity and Self-Identity: Self and Society in the Late Modern Age*. Cambridge: Polity.

Glaser, Barney, and Anselm Strauss. 1967. *The Discovery of Grounded Theory: Strategies for Qualitative Research*. Chicago: Aldine.

Gorz, André. 1985. *Paths to Paradise: On the Liberation from Work*. Trans. M. Imrie. Cambridge, Mass.: South End Press.

Granovetter, Mark. 1985. "Economic Action and Social Structure: The Problem of Embeddedness." *American Journal of Sociology* 91:481–510.

Hakim, Carol. 1993. "The Myth of Rising Female Employment." *Work, Employment, and Society* 7:97–120.

Harrison, Bennett. 1994. *Lean and Mean: The Changing Landscape of Corporate Power in the Age of Flexibility*. New York: Basic Books.

Hayden, Anders. 1999. *Sharing the Work, Sparing the Planet: Work Time, Consumption, and Ecology*. London: Zed Books.

Hays, Sharon. 1996. *The Cultural Contradictions of Motherhood*. New Haven: Yale University Press.

Hecksher, Charles. 1995. *White-Collar Blues*. New York: Basic Books.

Hochschild, Arlie Russell. 1989. *The Second Shift*. New York: Avon.

——. 1997. *The Time Bind: When Work Becomes Home and Home Becomes Work*. New York: Metropolitan Books.

Holcombe, Betty. 1998. *Not Guilty! The Good News about Working Mothers*. New York: Scribner.

Hunnicut, Benjamin Kline. 1988. *Work without End: Abandoning Shorter Hours for the Right to Work*. Philadelphia: Temple University Press.

Jacobs, Jerry, and Kathleen Gerson. 1998. "Who Are the Overworked Americans?" *Review of Social Economy* 56:442–59.

——. 2000. "Do Americans Feel Overworked? Comparing Ideal and Actual Working Time." In *Work and Family: Research Informing Policy*, ed. T. L. Parcel and D. B. Cornfield, pp. 71–95. Thousand Oaks, Calif.: Sage.

Kanter, Rosabeth Moss. 1977. *Men and Women of the Corporation*. New York: Basic Books.

Kidder, Tracy. 1982. *The Soul of a New Machine*. London: Allen & Unwin.

Kunda, Gideon. 1992. *Engineering Culture: Control and Commitment in a High-Tech Corporation*. Philadelphia: Temple University Press.

Larson, Magali Sarfatti. 1977. *The Rise of Professionalism: A Sociological Analysis.* Berkeley: University of California Press.

Levitan, Sar, and Elizabeth Conway. 1988. "Part-Timers: Living on Half-Rations." *Challenge*:9–16.

Lewicki, Roy, and Barbara Benedict Bunker. 1995. "Developing and Maintaining Trust in Work Relationships." In *Trust in Organizations: Frontiers of Theory and Research*, ed. R. Kramer and T. Tyler. Thousand Oaks, Calif.: Sage.

Lopata, Helena Z. 1994. *Circles and Settings: Role Changes of American Women.* Albany: SUNY Press.

Mackenzie, Donald. 1990. *Inventing Accuracy: A Historical Sociology of Nuclear Missile Guidance.* Cambridge: MIT Press.

Mangum, Garth, Donald Mayall, and Kristin Nelson. 1985. "The Temporary Help Industry: A Response to the Dual Internal Labor Market." *Industrial and Labor Relations Review* 38:599–611.

McIlwee, Judith, and J. Gregg Robinson. 1992. *Women in Engineering: Gender, Power, and Workplace Culture.* Albany: SUNY Press.

McKenney, James L., Michael H. Zack, and Victor S. Doherty. 1992. "Complementary Communication Media: A Comparison of Electronic Mail and Face-to-Face Communication in a Programming Team." In *Networks and Organizations: Structure, Form, and Action*, ed. N. Nohria and R. G. Eccles. Boston: Harvard Business School Press.

Meier, Greta S. 1978. *Job Sharing: A New Pattern for Quality of Work and Life.* Kalamazoo: W. E. Upjohn Institute for Employment Research.

Meiksins, Peter. 1988. "The Revolt of the Engineers Reconsidered." *Technology and Culture* 29:219–46.

Meiksins, Peter, and Peter Whalley. 2001. "Controlling Technical Workers in Alternative Work Arrangements." In *The Critical Study of Work: Labor, Technology, and Global Production*, ed. R. Baldoz, C. Koeber, and P. Kraft, pp. 236–57. Philadelphia: Temple University Press.

Mischler, Elliot. 1986. *Research Interviewing: Context and Narrative.* Cambridge: Harvard University Press.

Moen, Phyllis. 1985. "Continuities and Discontinuities in Women's Labor Force Activity." In *Life Course Dynamics: Trajectories and Transitions, 1968–1980*, ed. G. Elder, pp. 113–55. Ithaca: Cornell University Press.

Morgan, Gareth. 1986. *Images of Organization.* Beverly Hills: Sage.

Negrey, Cynthia. 1993. *Gender, Time, and Reduced Work.* Albany: SUNY Press.

Nippert-Eng, Christena. 1996. *Home and Work: Negotiating Boundaries through Everyday Life.* Chicago: University of Chicago Press.

Nohria, Nitin, and Robert Eccles. 1992. "Face-to-Face: Making Network Organizations Work." In *Network and Organizations: Structure, Form, and Action*, ed. N. Nohria and R. G. Eccles. Boston: Harvard Business School Press.

Nollen, Stanley D. 1982. *New Work Schedules in Practice*. New York: Van Nostrand Reinhold.

Olson, Margrethe. 1989. "Organizational Barriers to Professional Telework." In *Homework: Historical and Contemporary Perspectives on Paid Labor at Home*, ed. E. Boris and C. Daniels. Urbana: University of Illinois Press.

Osterman, Paul. 1988. *Employment Futures: Reorganization, Dislocation, and Public Policy*. New York: Oxford University Press.

Perlow, Leslie. 1997. *Finding Time: How Corporations, Individuals, and Families Can Benefit from New Work Practices*. Ithaca: ILR Press.

——. 2001. "Time to Coordinate: Toward an Understanding of Work-Time Standards and Norms in a Multicountry Study of Software Engineers." *Work and Occupations* 28: 91–111.

Pfeffer, Jeffrey, and James Baron. 1988. "Taking the Workers Back Out: Recent Trends in the Structuring of Employment." In *Research in Organizational Behavior* 10, ed. B. Staw and L. L. Cummings, pp. 257–303. Greenwich, Conn.: JAI Press.

Piore, Michael, and Charles Sabel. 1984. *The Second Industrial Divide*. New York: Basic Books.

Pleck, Joseph. 1993. "Are Family-Supportive Employer Policies Relevant to Men?" In *Men, Family, and Work*, ed. J. Hood, pp. 217–37. Newbury Park, Calif.: Sage.

Polivka, Anne E., and Thomas Nardone. 1989. "On the Definition of Contingent Work." *Monthly Labor Review* 112:9–16.

Potucheck, Jean. 1997. *Who Supports the Family? Gender and Breadwinning in Dual-Earner Marriages*. Stanford: Stanford University Press.

Putnam, Robert. 2000. *Bowling Alone: The Collapse and Revival of American Community*. New York: Simon & Schuster.

Quindlen, Anna. 1995. "Why I Quit." *Working Woman*, December, pp. 30–33.

Ricoeur, Paul. 1992. *Oneself as Another*. Trans. K. Blamey. Chicago: University of Chicago Press.

Rifkin, Jeremy. 1987. *Time Wars*. New York: Henry Holt.

——. 1995. *The End of Work: The Decline of the Global Force and the Dawn of the Post-Market Era*. New York: Putnam.

Robinson, John, and Geoffrey Godbey. 1997. *Time for Life: The Surprising Ways Americans Use Their Time*. University Park: Penn State University Press.

Ruskin, John. 1851. "Pre-Raphaelitism." In *The Oxford Book of Work*, ed. K. Thomas. Oxford: Oxford University Press.

Schor, Juliet. 1991. *The Overworked American: The Unexpected Decline of Leisure*. New York: Basic Books.

——. 1998. *The Overspent American: Upscaling, Downshifting, and the New Consumer*. New York: Basic Books.

Schwartz, Felice. 1989. "Management Women and the New Facts of Life." *Harvard Business Review* 67:65–76.

Seron, Carrol, and Kerry Ferris. 1995. "Negotiating Professionalism: Gendered Social Capital of Flexible Time." *Work and Occupations* 22:22–47.

Sirianni, Carmen. 1991. "The Self-Management of Time in Postindustrial Society." In *Working Time in Transition: The Political Economy of Working Hours in Industrial Nations,* ed. K. Hinrichs, W. Roch, and C. Sirianni. Philadelphia: Temple University Press.

Smith, Dorothy. 1987. *The Everyday World as Problematic: A Feminist Sociology.* Tonawanda: University of Toronto Press.

Smith, Vicki. 1990. *Managing in the Corporate Interest.* Berkeley: University of California Press.

——. 1997. "New Forms of Work Organization." *American Review of Sociology* 23:315–39.

Somers, Margaret R. 1994. "The Narrative Constitution of Identity: A Relational and Network Approach." *Theory and Society* 23:605–49.

Spradley, James P. 1979. *The Ethnographic Interview.* New York: Holt, Rinehart & Winston.

Sweeney, John, and Karen Nussbaum. 1989. *Solutions for the New Work Force.* Cabin John, Md.: Seven Locks Press.

Thompson, Jeffrey, and J. Stuart Bunderson. 2001. "Work/Non-Work Conflict and the Phenomenology of Time." *Work and Occupations* 28:17–39.

Tilly, Chris. 1991. "Reasons for the Continuing Growth of Part-Time Employment." *Industrial Relations* 31:330–47.

——. 1996. *Half A Job: Bad and Good Part-Time Jobs in a Changing Labor Market.* Philadelphia: Temple University Press.

Useem, Jerry. 2000. "Welcome to the New Company Town." *Fortune,* Jan. 10, 2000, pp. 62–70.

Whalley, Peter. 1986a. *The Social Production of Technical Work.* Albany: SUNY Press.

——. 1986b. "Markets, Managers, and Technical Autonomy." *Theory and Society* 15:223–47.

Williams, Joan. 2000. *Unbending Gender: Why Family and Work Conflict and What to Do about It.* Oxford: Oxford University Press.

Williamson, Oliver. 1974. *Markets and Hierarchies: Analysis of Antitrust Implications.* Glencoe, Ill.: Free Press.

Yakura, Elaine. 2001. "Billables: The Valorization of Time in Consulting." *American Behavioral Scientist* 44:1076–95.

Zerubavel, Eviator. 1987. "The Language of Time: Toward a Semiotics of Temporality." *Sociological Quarterly* 28:343–56.

Index